BENSENVILLE COMMUNITY PUBLIC LIBRARY

3 1437 00483 0995

Bensenville Community Public Library
Bensenville. IL 60106

P9-BBT-418

Bensenville Community Public Library
Bensenville, IL 60106

STERLING BIOGRAPHIES

ANNE FRANK

Hidden Hope

Rita Thievon Mullin

STERLING

New York / London
www.sterlingpublishing.com/kids

To Laura, the newest member of our family.

And, in memory of Peter Mayer, who escaped Nazi Germany as a child and inspired a generation of American college students.

Thanks to the librarians at the U.S. Holocaust Memorial Museum for their help in accessing interviews with Holocaust survivors, and to my editor, Susan Hoe, for her guidance in shaping the manuscript. Special thanks to Michael, Matt, and Laura Mullin, who read each chapter and offered me invaluable comments along the way.

The portions of Anne Frank's diary quoted throughout the text of this book are from THE DIARY OF A YOUNG GIRL THE DEFINITIVE EDITION by Anne Frank, edited by Otto H. Frank and Mirjam Pressler, translated by Susan Massotty, translation copyright © 1995 by Doubleday, a division of Random House, Inc. Used by permission of Doubleday, a division of Random House, Inc.

STERLING and the distinctive Sterling logo are registered trademarks of Sterling Publishing Co., Inc.

Library of Congress Cataloging-in-Publication Data

Mullin, Rita T.
  Anne Frank : hidden hope / Rita Thievon Mullin.
     p. cm. — (Sterling biographies)
  Includes bibliographical references and index.
  ISBN 978-1-4027-5148-6 (pbk.) — ISBN 978-1-4027-6539-1 (hardcover)
  1. Frank, Anne, 1929-1945—Juvenile literature. 2. Jewish children in the Holocaust—
Netherlands—Amsterdam—Biography—Juvenile literature. 3. Holocaust, Jewish (1939-1945)—
Netherlands—Amsterdam—Biography—Juvenile literature. I. Title.
  DS135.N6F734975 2008
  940.53'18092—dc22
  [B]
                                2008028922

10 9 8 7 6 5 4 3 2 1

Published by Sterling Publishing Co., Inc.
387 Park Avenue South, New York, NY 10016

© 2009 by Rita Thievon Mullin

Distributed in Canada by Sterling Publishing
c/o Canadian Manda Group, 165 Dufferin Street
Toronto, Ontario, Canada M6K 3H6
Distributed in the United Kingdom by GMC Distribution Services
Castle Place, 166 High Street, Lewes, East Sussex, England BN7 1XU
Distributed in Australia by Capricorn Link (Australia) Pty. Ltd.
P.O. Box 704, Windsor, NSW 2756, Australia

Printed in China

All rights reserved

Sterling ISBN 987-1-4027-5148-6 (paperback)
          ISBN 978-1-4027-6539-1 (hardcover)

Image research by Larry Schwartz

For information about custom editions, special sales, premium and corporate purchases, please contact Sterling Special Sales Department at 800-805-5489 or specialsales@sterlingpublishing.com.

Contents

Bensenville Community Public Library
Bensenville, IL 60106

INTRODUCTION: Anne's Prized Gift 1

CHAPTER 1: Born in the Shadow of War 2

CHAPTER 2: A New Life in Amsterdam 12

CHAPTER 3: Making the Most of Difficult Times 25

CHAPTER 4: Vanishing into Thin Air 40

CHAPTER 5: Life in Hiding 47

CHAPTER 6: Living with Fear 64

CHAPTER 7: An Author in the Making 73

CHAPTER 8: Hope Betrayed 79

CHAPTER 9: From the Annex to the Camps 88

CHAPTER 10: The Aftermath 105

CHAPTER 11: What Happened to the Others? 113

GLOSSARY 116

BIBLIOGRAPHY 117

SOURCE NOTES 118

IMAGE CREDITS 122

ABOUT THE AUTHOR 122

INDEX 123

Events in the Life of Anne Frank

1929

June 12, 1929
Anne Frank is born in
Frankfurt-on-Main, Germany,
to Otto and Edith Frank.

1933
Adolf Hitler is named
chancellor of Germany.

February 1934
Anne joins her family in
Amsterdam, the Netherlands,
to escape Germany.

September 1, 1939
Germany invades Poland. World
War II begins two days later.

May 10, 1940
Germany invades the
Netherlands.

Fall 1941
Jewish children in the Netherlands
are forbidden to attend school
with non-Jews. Anne and her
sister, Margot, begin attending
the Jewish Lyceum.

April 1942
All Jews in the Netherlands
are required to wear a yellow
six-sided star in public.

June 12, 1942
Anne receives a diary for her
thirteenth birthday.

July 6, 1942
Frank family goes into hiding in
secret rooms above Otto Frank's
business. Days later, the Van
Pelses join the Franks in hiding.

November 1942
Fritz Pfeffer is allowed to share
the hiding place in the annex
with the Franks and Van Pelses.

April 1944
Anne begins revising
her diary for possible
publication after the war.

June 6, 1944
Allies land at Normandy,
France, on D-Day.

August 1, 1944
Anne writes her final diary entry.

August 4, 1944
The Franks, Van Pelses, and
Pfeffer are found and arrested
by Nazis.

September 3, 1944
The Franks, Van Pelses, and
Pfeffer board the last train
from Westerbork to Auschwitz,
the most notorious Nazi
concentration camp.

October 30, 1944
Anne and Margot Frank are sent
to the Bergen-Belsen camp in
Germany.

January 27, 1945
Soviet troops liberate
Auschwitz. Otto Frank is one of
the few surviving prisoners there.

1945–1947
In March 1945, Margot and Anne
Frank die of typhus. In May
1945, Allies declare victory in
Europe. In March 1947, Anne
Frank's diary is published in the
Netherlands.

1947

Anne's Prized Gift

I still believe, in spite of everything, that people are truly good at heart . . .

Anne Frank's most prized gift on her thirteenth birthday in 1942 was a red-and-white-checked diary. Only weeks later, she would pack it into her small bag of possessions and carry it with her when she went into hiding from the **Nazis** during World War II. For the next two years, her family and others hid silently above her father's business in Amsterdam, avoiding arrest and shipment to **concentration camps** in Germany and Poland, where millions of Jews and other people were cruelly treated and killed by the Nazis.

After two years in hiding, Anne wrote in her diary, "It's a wonder I haven't abandoned all my ideals. . . . I cling to them, because I still believe, in spite of everything, that people are truly good at heart. . . . I hear the approaching thunder, . . . I feel the sufferings of millions. And yet, . . . I feel that everything will change for the better, that this cruelty too will end, [and] that peace and tranquility will return once more."

Anne Frank's diary has helped people the world over to understand the impact of hatred on its victims and has opened dialogues in classrooms and government halls about the awful price of prejudice. Her story is as moving—and her words are as relevant—today as they were more than a half-century ago.

CHAPTER 1

Born in the Shadow of War

[Anne was] a little rebel with a will of her own.
  —Otto Frank

Anne Frank announced her presence to the world at full volume. She began crying soon after her birth in Frankfurt-on-Main, Germany, on June 12, 1929, and cried for weeks afterward, making sleepless nights the rule for her parents, Otto and Edith Frank. She was the second of two daughters. The first, Margot, was three-and-a-half when Anne was born. Margot had been a quiet, serene baby, so Anne's bold approach to life came as a surprise.

Anne Frank was born in 1929 in Frankfurt, Germany, where the family lived until Anne was four. The Frankfurt neighborhood is shown in this 1957 photograph.

Otto and Edith were devoted parents who understood that their two daughters were as different as they were. Margot was much like her mother: intelligent, shy, hardworking, and respectful. Anne was much like her father: curious, social, and lively; she was a child who loved to be the center of attention.

When Margot and Anne were babies, Otto Frank worked for a small Frankfurt bank started by his father. Born in 1889, he had grown up in a well-to-do family and attended Heidelberg University. After only a semester there, he left and traveled to New York. He took a job at Macy's department store, which was owned by the father of his friend Nathan Straus, Jr. The two had met at Heidelberg University and remained friends for life. Otto loved the big, lively city, but he returned to Germany after only a few months when his father died suddenly.

Born in 1900, Edith Frank was the youngest child of Abraham and Rosa Stern Hollander. Her father was a wealthy manufacturer in Aachen, Germany, on the border of Belgium and the Netherlands. Edith remembered her privileged childhood fondly. After she and Otto married in 1925, Edith devoted herself to making a comfortable home for her husband and daughters.

Anne Frank's parents, Edith and Otto, pose for a wedding portrait with their guests on May 12, 1925, in Aachen, Germany.

Imaginary Friends

Otto later recalled that through her preschool years Anne was "a little rebel with a will of her own. She was often wakeful at night." He would go into her room "many times, petting her and singing nursery songs" to settle her back to sleep.

Anne and her family lived in an apartment on the edge of Frankfurt in western Germany. Frankfurt is a center of German industry and trade, and in the 1920s, it had the second-largest Jewish population in Germany after Berlin, the capital. The Franks were among some thirty thousand Jews living in the city.

Their apartment was part of a house that had a small backyard. The neighborhood had many young families, so finding friends to play with was never a problem for Margot and Anne. The neighborhood children gathered to play in the backyard on the swing and in the sandbox. Anne loved to follow along behind her older sister and the other children.

At the end of days playing, Margot seemed untouched by the dirt and sand, but Anne would be covered in mud. Kati Stilgenbauer, the Franks' housekeeper, remembered going out onto the apartment's balcony one day where Anne, then a toddler, was splashing and laughing as she sat in a puddle in the rain. Kati tried to scold her and make her come inside, but Anne insisted that Kati tell her a story first. When Kati said she was much too busy to tell a dirty little girl a story, Anne told her she could make it a short one.

Tell Me a Story

Anne loved stories. Above her changing table in the nursery hung a lamp painted with animals. Her parents would tell her stories about them as they changed her clothes. From the time she could talk, she would make up stories about the same painted animals.

Storytelling was a Frank family tradition. Each night, Otto Frank would tell his daughters a bedtime story. Their favorites were ones about Good Paula and Bad Paula. According to the tale, the two Paulas had come to live in the nursery before Anne was born.

Margot (left) and Anne Frank (center) sit on their father Otto's lap in Frankfurt, Germany, in 1931. Anne kept this picture in her photo album.

Good Paula would always eat the vegetables on her plate and would happily share her toys with others, but Bad Paula would make faces as she pushed the vegetables around her plate and would pull the hair of other children when no one was looking. Margot always knew which Paula she preferred. Anne loved the imaginary girls, too. She knew that she should favor Good Paula, but at times, she admired Bad Paula's spirit—if only just a little.

The Rising Tide of Hatred

In the 1920s, Germany was bent beneath the burden of having lost World War I (1914–1918) in the previous decade. During that war, the Central powers of Germany, Austro-Hungary, and Turkey fought against the Allied forces of France, Great Britain, Russia, Italy, and (after 1917) the United States. Otto Frank and many other Jewish men bravely fought for their country. The war devastated Europe, particularly the Central powers. More than eight million soldiers and more than thirteen million civilians died of injuries or illness on both sides during the war.

The war and the economic punishments placed on Germany by the victorious Allies left the country's economy in shambles.

German soldiers advance through smoke and fire near Somme, France, in 1918, during World War I. The German surge was short lived. The war ended with an Allied victory in November 1918.

With rising prices and few jobs, many German families had great difficulty putting food on the table and keeping a roof over their heads. In that chaos, people searched for someone to blame for their problems and for someone who could lift them from the turmoil and poverty.

The National Socialist German Workers' Party (known more commonly as the Nazi Party), led by Adolf Hitler, capitalized on workers' frustrations, wounded national pride, and the **anti-Semitism** that lingered beneath the surface of German society. He blamed many of the nation's ills on Jews and described a "master race" of ethnic Germans who would

Adolf Hitler's dramatic speaking style attracted many to the Nazi Party. In this 1925 photograph, Hitler rehearses a speech before a camera to study how his gestures would look before a crowd.

Spreading the Seeds of Destruction

Prejudice and discrimination against Jews, called anti-Semitism, goes back nearly two thousand years, when Roman soldiers drove the Jews from the land that is now Israel. The Jews spread throughout the world, trying to live their faith as a minority, often in the Christian countries of Europe.

In the late nineteenth century, as Europe established colonies in Africa and Asia, some European politicians began spreading the idea that the white race was superior to all others, including Jews, whom they mistakenly labeled as a race. In Austria and Germany, this idea took particular hold. Karl Lueger, who became mayor of Vienna, Austria, late in the century, blamed Jews for the city's economic problems. A young man named Adolf Hitler lived there and took Lueger's hatred to heart.

Politician Karl Lueger is satirized in this 1892 political cartoon. In it, he asks, "Do I look like I would eat Jews?" while grabbing a caricature of a Jew. Lueger's anti-Semitism influenced young Adolf Hitler.

someday conquer the world. Hitler's dramatic speeches at first seemed ridiculous to many German citizens. He was, they said, a crazy man to whom no one would listen. In the 1920s, however, his rhetoric caught fire with working class Germans and **hooligans** who found a home with the party's paramilitary **Brown Shirts**, or Storm Troopers.

A New Part of Town

By 1932, the Nazi Party had the largest voting block in the Reichstag, the national lawmaking body. By the following year the party had taken control of the Reichstag, and Hitler was named **chancellor** of Germany. Soon afterward, Hitler became **dictator** of the German people, crushing opponents and pursuing his plans to dominate the world.

Adolf Hitler shakes hands with Paul Von Hindenberg, president of Germany, after Hitler is appointed chancellor of Germany in 1933. Within months, Hitler becomes Germany's dictator.

A group of Nazi paramilitary Brown Shirts, or Storm Troopers, stands in front of the Worker's Bank in Berlin after arresting all the labor leaders inside in May 1933.

Hitler's hate-filled message soon touched the Frank family personally. Their landlord, Mr. Konitzer, was a Nazi **sympathizer**, and his cruel remarks against Jews, as well as the anti-Semitic songs of gangs of Brown Shirts who would march down their street, made life unbearable. In 1931, when Anne was nearly two years old, the Franks decided to leave their apartment. They also needed to find a less expensive place to live. Like most other Germans, they were learning to make do with less than they had in the past. The family business was not doing well, and money was tight. The family moved to a ground-floor apartment in an old villa in a nearby neighborhood that, for a time, was free of such **rabble-rousing**.

Otto Frank was convinced that the crazed ranting of Adolf Hitler could no longer be ignored. Those who opposed the party were being attacked. In March 1933, the mayor of Frankfurt, an ethnic Jew and opponent of the Nazis, resigned and fled the city in fear for his safety. The Franks realized that many of their Christian friends had stopped calling or visiting them.

In early 1933, the Franks moved again, this time to live with Otto's mother in the large, comfortable family home in Frankfurt. The Franks made great efforts to protect Margot and Anne from the ugly realities of what was happening, but soon the girls felt the effects first hand. In April 1933, Jewish teachers and those who opposed the Nazis could no longer teach in public schools. Margot was segregated with the other Jewish students in a corner of the classroom. Anne, who had been scheduled to begin kindergarten in the fall, would not be allowed to attend a public school.

Otto and Edith Frank made plans to flee Germany. But where would they go? How would Otto Frank support his family? With the help of Erich Elias, his sister Leni's husband, Otto set up a branch of Opekta, a company that sold pectin, an ingredient needed for making jellies and jams, in Amsterdam, the Netherlands. The Elias family had already fled Germany and was living in Switzerland. Otto's brother Robert and his wife had moved to London.

Otto and Edith Frank made plans to flee Germany. But where would they go?

In August 1933, the borders between Germany and the Netherlands were still open. Otto Frank went to Amsterdam to set up his business. The Netherlands had remained neutral during World War I, siding with neither the Allied nor Central powers, and he believed that his family would be safe there even if another war broke out.

While Otto worked to establish the business, Edith, Margot, and Anne stayed in Aachen, Germany, with Edith's mother, Rosa Hollander, and her two brothers, Julius and Walter. Aachen is

Five-year-old Anne Frank poses in a photo booth in Aachen, Germany, in 1934. The photo also gives her weight in kilograms, which is equivalent to 54 pounds.

located on the German border near the Netherlands. There the family was much closer to Amsterdam than they had been in Frankfurt.

Anne continued to be a lively, curious little girl who was not afraid to speak her mind. Like many youngest children who hate being the "baby," Anne loved seeing children younger than she was. "She peeks into every pram we pass. If she had her way, she would take every toddler she sees for a walk," her mother wrote to a friend.

Anne did not only feel protective of babies. When she was only four, she boarded a crowded **streetcar** with Grandma Hollander. All the seats were taken. "Won't someone offer a seat to this old lady?" she called out. Her sense of justice and her concern for her beloved grandmother would not let her be silent.

Margot and Anne enjoyed the summer and fall in Aachen as Edith made several trips to Amsterdam to help Otto find an apartment for the family. Soon the family would be together again—in a country still untouched by Nazi terror.

CHAPTER 2

A New Life in Amsterdam

When she played the queen or the princess she suddenly seemed a good bit taller than the others.

—Hendrika Kuperus, Anne's schoolteacher

When Edith Frank joined Otto in Amsterdam in late 1933 to set up a comfortable home for their family in their new country, Anne and Margot stayed behind in Germany with Grandma Hollander. In December, Margot joined her parents in Amsterdam so that she could settle into their new country before school began in early January. Anne, who had not yet started school, stayed behind a bit longer.

Margot's eighth birthday on February 16, 1934, was her first in the Netherlands. She had made a few friends at

Margot Frank carries a small overnight bag as she visits her grandmother, Rosa Hollander, in Aachen, Germany, in May 1929, a month before the birth of her sister, Anne.

Margot (back row, right) and Anne (front row, left) pose with Margot's new friends at her eighth birthday party in Amsterdam on February 16, 1934. The family had recently moved there.

her new school, but the Dutch language still seemed a confusing jumble of sounds. She also missed her sister, who was still in Aachen.

On that day, as Margot walked into the living room to see the gifts piled on a table, she found the best present of all: her sister Anne, dressed in a white tutu, laughing and squealing at the sight of Margot. The family was together again.

The normally lively Anne quietly watched Margot's new friends at the party, clinging to her father as she adjusted to her new surroundings. But soon, she returned to her old, bubbly self. Four months later, by her fifth birthday party, Anne was already speaking more than a few words of Dutch and had made friends of her own.

A New Home

In the spring, Anne began attending kindergarten at the Montessori school nearby. There she became instant best friends with Hannah Goslar. Like the Franks, the Goslars were a Jewish family who had recently fled from Germany. The families had met during the first week the Goslars were in the Netherlands, before Hannah started school.

When Hannah arrived at school on her first day, the girls spotted each other across the room. Hannah was delighted to see a familiar face and hear her native language. They greeted each other with hugs like long-lost friends. Anne helped Hannah adjust to her new school. Their friendship continued at home. Luckily, Hannah's family lived in the same building on the floor below. The second of Anne's closest friends was Susanne Lederman. Everyone called her Sanne (pronounced "Sannah"). Like the Franks and Goslars, her family, who was also Jewish, had recently **emigrated** from Germany. Sanne, the quietest of the three, lived around the corner and attended a different school nearby. Outside school, the three girls were inseparable: "Here come Anna, Sanne, and Hannah," people would say as the three walked down the street.

Anne (right) jumps rope as her friend Sanne Lederman (left), plays with a hoop on the sidewalk near Anne's home in Amsterdam in 1935. Neighborhood children played there by the hour.

Merwede Square, where the Franks' apartment was located, was an L-shaped development of apartments joined by a twelve-story "skyscraper" in the River Quarter of Amsterdam. The new neighborhood became a magnet for immigrants from Germany and elsewhere looking for a place to live. It was still under construction, and the children took advantage of the over-sized construction-site "sandbox" for playing. Later, the grassy plaza that replaced the dirt and sand became the neighborhood's gathering place.

When children wanted to play, they would go to each other's front door and instead of knocking or ringing the bell, they would lift the cover of the mail slot in the door and whistle. Poor Anne! No matter how hard she tried, she could not whistle. But that did not stop her. She would simply lift the cover and sing, "la-la-la-la-la." Everyone knew when Anne had come to call.

Their days were filled with playing hopscotch, hide-and-seek, and tag and turning cartwheels and handstands on the grass. Anne was no better at acrobatics than at whistling. "She always sagged at once, lost her balance, and tumbled over," her friend Toosje remembered. Perhaps the reason for her clumsiness was her shoulder, which she could pop out of its socket at will to entertain or shock the other children. She was also not above a bit of mischief. She and Hannah would occasionally throw water out the window of the Franks' third-floor apartment on passersby below.

School Days

The Montessori school that Anne attended encouraged children to work independently and at their own pace. The school was perfect for Anne. She could get up and move around or talk to other students whenever she needed to—and she often needed to.

Anne Frank is seated in front of the teacher, Mrs. Baldal, in this 1937 photograph of her Montessori school class. Anne attended the school from 1934 until 1941.

After kindergarten, Anne continued at the Montessori school, to which she walked each day. Her teacher for her first several years there was Jan van Gelder. He and Anne often walked to school in the mornings together. He remembered the stories and poems she would recite for him—some told to her by her father, others made up by Anne herself. Their walks passed quickly with Anne talking constantly, hardly stopping for breath.

Despite her lively imagination, Anne was no model student. She did well only in the subjects that interested her. She loved reading and history, but arithmetic always baffled her. Anne was also often sick, which made keeping up with her math skills more difficult.

In December 1936, their third year in school, Hannah came down with measles, and five days later Anne had broken out with them too—the only two children in the class to sprout those telltale red spots. Anne also had a heart condition, and between the measles and her heart problems, she missed weeks of school that year. Because of her heart, she had to sit out during

Montessori Schools

The Montessori school that Anne attended was a special type of school developed by Italian educator Dr. Maria Montessori early in the twentieth century. The school ran on an educational philosophy that allowed children to work independently at their own pace. There are many Montessori schools in operation today, in which children do hands-on activities, using all five senses, to learn concepts such as mathematics and science. Activities are based on children's developmental levels, not necessarily their age or grade.

Italian educator Maria Montessori established the first school using her methods in 1907. There, teaching is based on children's developmental level and natural curiosity, not their age.

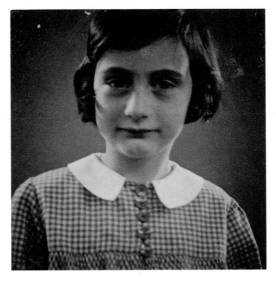

Anne kept this copy of her passport photo, taken in May 1936. This photo would have been on her passport when she left Germany for the Netherlands the following winter.

gym class, and rough sports were forbidden, too. She loved to swim, though, which was not as hard on her body, and she once won two medals for swimming at a local pool.

Although Anne could not take part in most athletic activities, she found her calling in her fifth year at the Montessori school. The classes began producing short plays. Anne helped write some of them, and with her gift for drama, she was a natural performer. "She was rather small among her schoolmates," Mrs. Kuperus, her teacher, remembered, "but when she played the queen or the princess she suddenly seemed a good bit taller than the others."

The Center of Life

The center of life for Anne and Margot was the family's apartment at 37 Merwede Square. It was spacious enough that the family could rent out a room to lodgers. It was also centrally heated, which was a luxury at the time, making it cozy even during Amsterdam's cold, damp winters. But more than that, Edith Frank created a home for the family there that combined the best of their old life in Germany with new hope for the future.

The apartment was filled with lovely, comfortable furniture, including some antiques from Edith's childhood home. She especially treasured a small desk and grandfather clock that visitors admired. There were also bookcases overflowing with volumes collected by both parents.

However, this home was not a fussy museum piece. Children's toys and books were scattered about, and neighborhood children were regular guests. Edith served biscuits topped with cream or jam to hungry visitors after school. One child who regularly stopped by was Julianne Duke, who lived on the floor above them. Years later, she fondly remembered Mrs. Frank's cream-cheese sandwiches topped with chocolate sprinkles. Anne was constantly inviting friends to join them for dinner. At the Frank home, children were equal partners in the dinner conversation at a time when children in other homes were expected to be seen and not heard.

The center of life for Anne and Margot was the family's apartment at 37 Merwede Square.

Unlike many of the other children's fathers, who were serious and not very outgoing with children, Otto Frank delighted in his daughters and their friends. "When he entered a room, the sun began to shine," remembered Hannah. Otto listened eagerly to the children's tales and told stories and jokes of his own. Everyone knew that he had a special place in his heart for Anne. She could be difficult, and at times unpredictable, but he could always manage her moods with a quiet word or a firm-but-gentle reminder.

Anne and Hannah were particularly close. Their two families would spend Friday evenings together to celebrate the beginning of the Jewish **Sabbath**, called *Shabbat*. Their mothers, Hannah later remembered, were very close. Although Otto was not religious, Edith was, and she attended religious services regularly. Margot shared her interest in religion and began studying Hebrew. Anne, like her father, had little concern for religion, but celebrated the Jewish holidays with the Goslars.

Anne also joined the Goslars on summer holidays. Above her bed at home, she hung a photo of the hotel cottage near the North Sea where she had vacationed with them. The girls had spent a day at an amusement park there, laughing at their strange reflections in the hall of mirrors and carrying home souvenir piggy banks they watched being made. One evening, while Mr. and Mrs. Goslar were out for a walk and the girls were in the cottage alone, a fierce storm came up, with ear-shattering thunder and a fireworks display of lightning across the sky. Anne began to cry, feeling frightened and homesick. Although she was happy again in the morning, her nighttime fears would continue even as she grew older.

Building a Business

As Anne and Margot were becoming proper young women, Otto was working constantly to build a business to support his family. His company, called Opekta, sold pectin to housewives who needed it to make jelly and jam from berries in season. His office had expanded to include two office workers. He hired Victor Kugler to manage the office. Very different from the warm, smiling Otto Frank, Kugler was precise about how things were done. Assisting them both was Hermine "Miep" Santrouschitz, who seemed to handle every office task, from making the coffee and sending out bills to mastering jelly and jam making in the office kitchen so that she could help customers who called or wrote when their jellies or jams came out wrong.

Miep and her boyfriend Jan Gies soon became regular guests in the Franks' home and favorites of Anne's. Austrian by birth, Miep had lived in Holland with foster parents from the age of eleven. Like the Franks, she spoke German and Dutch, but unlike Mr. and Mrs. Frank, who still struggled with Dutch, she was fluent in both. Jan was a social worker for the city government. Both Miep and Jan shared the Franks' political opinions. They were

Hermine "Miep" Santrouschitz (later Gies) joined Otto Frank's business as a secretary. She soon mastered jam making in order to answer customers' questions.

horrified by what was happening in Germany under the Nazis and feared what might occur in their own country in the future.

Otto often traveled throughout Holland for days at a time. He was trying to find new clients, usually drug stores, to stock his products. "My husband is hardly ever at home," Edith wrote to a friend. "Work is getting harder and harder." In 1935, business began to improve. He hired several women to demonstrate how to use the product in making jams and jellies and employed several men in the warehouse to fill orders.

Jelly making is a summertime activity. To keep his business thriving year 'round, in 1938, Otto started a second business: Pectacon sold spices largely

> *Both Miep and Jan. . . . were horrified by what was happening in Germany under the Nazis and feared what might occur in their own country in the future.*

used in sausages, which were made in cooler weather. He hired an old friend, Johannes Kleiman, to work in the office. Jo Kleiman, as everyone called him, had worked with Otto at the Frank family bank years earlier. He became a director and bookkeeper for both businesses.

Otto also hired Hermann van Pels, a spice expert. Miep recalled that "there was nothing about spices [he] didn't know; with one sniff of his nose he could name any spice."

The Darkening Shadow of Anti-Semitism

Otto made his last business trip back to Germany in 1938, where life for Jews was becoming impossible under the Nazis. The Nuremberg Laws, passed in 1935, essentially legalized Nazi

A sign reading, "Germans, defend yourselves, do not buy from Jews," is posted in front of a store owned by Jews in Berlin. Nazis announced the boycott of Jewish businesses in April 1933.

anti-Semitism, and "No Jews Allowed" signs were appearing in stores and restaurants throughout Germany. Those people that the state defined as Jews were stripped of their German citizenship and forbidden to marry non-Jews.

As conditions in Germany worsened, Edith and Otto began to fear that their flight from Germany had not been far enough to escape the Nazis' grip, but they could not agree on whether to leave—or where to go. The Franks and their friends kept their fears and concerns from their children as much as possible. When youngsters walked into the room as the adults shared after-dinner coffee, the grown-up conversation slipped easily from worries about politics to questions about the children's schoolwork or holidays. The girls' lives remained relatively unshaken by what was happening in the world.

But Margot, who was three years older than Anne, was becoming increasingly aware of the threats to their peaceful lives. Around this time the girls both found American pen pals. While Anne's letters were carefree, Margot's referred to the darkening political horizon.

Margot's 1939 passport photo was kept by Anne in her photo album. Margot was thirteen years old and an excellent student. She was a serious-minded girl who loved to read and do crossword puzzles.

Anne's American Pen Pal

In the summer of 1939, Birdie Mathews, a teacher in Iowa, met some teachers from Anne Frank's school while traveling in Europe. They gave her a list of students who were interested in having American pen pals. That fall, Juanita Wagner, who lived on a farm in Danville, Iowa, chose Anne Frank's name from the list and wrote to her immediately. Anne wrote back in April 1940. She drafted her letter in Dutch, then Otto translated it into English, and Anne copied it for her new friend. She enclosed a picture of herself and a picture postcard of Amsterdam. Margot began writing to Juanita's older sister, Betty. Juanita and Betty wrote back to Anne and Margot immediately, sending pictures of themselves. They never received replies from the girls. By the time their letters would have reached the Netherlands, the country had been invaded by Germany. The letters do not seem to have reached Amsterdam.

This photo shows Juanita Wagner, Anne Frank's American pen pal, in 1940, the year she and Anne exchanged letters. Juanita lived on a farm in Danville, Iowa.

CHAPTER 3

Making the Most of Difficult Times

Memories mean more to me than dresses.

On September 1, 1939, Germany invaded Poland. Two days later, Britain and France declared war on Germany. World War II had begun. Only eight months later, on May 10, 1940, Germany invaded the Netherlands. On that Friday morning, citizens of the Netherlands were awakened by the news. In Amsterdam the drone of warplanes overhead convinced the townspeople that the radio reports were true. The city was eerily quiet. Families kept their children home from school, waiting to see what would happen.

A curfew required everyone to be off the streets at 8:00 at night. Families were urged to cover their windows with blackout paper to prevent any light from giving German planes a beacon for attack.

Soldiers watch Rotterdam, the second largest city in the Netherlands, burn after German bombing in May 1940. Rotterdam was almost completely destroyed. The Dutch surrendered to the Germans the following day.

Many Jews who had fled Germany only a few years earlier panicked, some rushing to ports and train stations. A few were lucky enough to escape, but most returned home when they found that the few ships at port were already full, and the roads out of the country were already blocked by German soldiers. Still others, like the Franks, stayed at home. They knew that any successful escape would have to be more carefully planned.

Rationing cards had been distributed by the government months earlier, after Germany had invaded Poland. In the weeks after the invasion of the Netherlands, the cards limited the basic foods families could buy to ensure that people did not hoard food, making others go hungry, and to guarantee enough food supplies for the military.

Only four days after the invasion, the Dutch government surrendered. Queen Wilhelmina and her advisors fled to England. As German troops marched through the city, life began returning to normal. Businesses reopened, and children returned to school.

Dutch Queen Wilhelmina (left), Prince Consort Bernhard, holding Princess Beatrix (center), and Princess Juliana (right) leaving their palace. They fled to England shortly after the German invasion to run a Dutch government in exile.

Although the Franks continued to shield Anne and Margot as much as they could, the invasion quickly intruded on every aspect of life. Anne's eleventh birthday on June 12 was approaching, and she was unhappy that her party would be more modest than in years past. The invasion also meant that she could no longer visit her Grandmother Frank and her cousins in neutral Switzerland, where her family had spent many happy vacations.

The Noose Tightens

By July, all people under German rule were forbidden to listen to the British Broadcasting Company (BBC) or to Radio Orange, a station established by the Dutch government in exile in England. Radio Orange carried nightly broadcasts, including addresses by Queen Wilhelmina, to encourage and reassure Dutch citizens.

At first, the changes to life caused by the German invasion seemed small and they applied to all Dutch citizens. Soon, though, the impact on Jews alone was obvious. Books by Jewish authors disappeared from school library shelves, and citizens, fearful of German searches, threw them away from their home libraries as well. In August, German Jews who had arrived in Holland after 1932 had to register with the government. In October 1940, businesses with more than twenty-five percent Jewish ownership also had to be registered.

Otto Frank responded swiftly. He asked Miep's fiancé, Jan Gies, a non-Jew, to form a company to officially take over Pectacon, Otto's spice business. Their action protected Pectacon from being taken over by the German-controlled government. Pectacon became Gies and Company, and Otto's office manager, Victor Kugler, became director. In the same way, Opekta, the pectin company, was headed by Otto's old friend and colleague Jo Kleiman, also a non-Jew. In reality, however, Otto Frank continued to run both companies.

In 1940, business began picking up. In December, the companies moved to a new location: 263 Prinsengracht (Prince's Canal). The building was actually made up of two back-to-back buildings. The warehouse covered the ground floor in both buildings. The front building had offices and storage on the floors above. The back building had an office and kitchen on the first floor above the warehouse, and the floors above that were largely empty.

At first, the changes to life caused by the German invasion seemed small. . . . Soon, though, the impact on Jews alone was obvious.

By January 1941, all Jews, including lifelong Netherlanders, had to register with the government—even if they had only one grandparent who was Jewish. The order for Jews to register convinced Otto and Edith that they must make plans to escape. The year before, Otto had written to Milly Stanfield, his cousin in England, about his fears that Germany would invade the Netherlands. "I don't know what to do about the children. I can't talk to Edith about it. There's no use worrying her before she has to be worried." Milly offered to care for the girls in England during the war. Otto and Edith discussed the plan, but they could not bear the thought of separating the family. Whatever the future held, it would happen to them together.

In 1941, Otto worked feverishly to secure **visas** to the United States for the family. He acted through his old college friend Nathan Straus, Jr., who was then head of the U.S. Housing Authority, and Edith's two brothers, Julius and Walter, who had fled to America earlier.

By the time Otto made these desperate efforts, though, entering the United States from the Netherlands had become nearly impossible. The two countries would soon be at war.

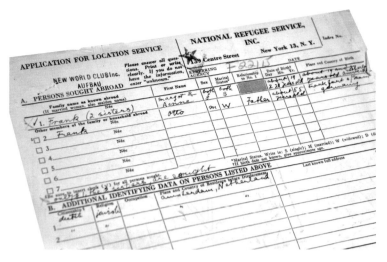

Otto Frank filled out many forms, including these, when attempting to resettle his family in the United States in 1941. His efforts failed, and the family remained in the Netherlands.

The Frank family's fate would have to be played out in the Netherlands.

Trying to Maintain a Normal Life

Otto and Edith continued to keep their political discussions and personal plans from the girls. They did not want them to be robbed of their childhoods any sooner than necessary. They celebrated Margot's fifteenth birthday on February 16, 1941, and Anne's twelfth birthday on June 12 with the same generosity as always. Anne received a new bicycle, which gave her a precious measure of freedom.

The girls continued to attend their schools, but the government banned many free-time activities for Jews. In the spring, Jews were forbidden to go to movie theaters. In May, Jews were no longer permitted to enter public parks or swimming pools. Anne seemed to take it in stride. She wrote to her Grandmother Frank in Switzerland that summer, saying "We don't have much chance to get tanned any more because we can't go to the swimming pool. It's a pity, but that's how it is."

Otto and Edith continued to keep their political discussions and personal plans from the girls.

But the summer brought two happy occasions. Anne went with Sanne's family to a summerhouse owned by relatives of the Ledermans. The house, only about fifty miles from Amsterdam, seemed a world away from the city's nighttime rumble of aircraft and regular air-raid sirens. "We sleep a lot better at night here than in Amsterdam," she wrote to her Grandmother Frank. "There's nothing at all to disturb us."

On July 16, 1941, Miep and Jan were married. Otto and Anne joined the happy wedding party at City Hall. Margot and Grandma Hollander, who was by then living with them, were

Wedding guests of Miep and Jan Gies outside the courthouse for the ceremony on July 17, 1941. Left to right: Laurens and Anna Nieuwenberg (Miep's foster parents), Otto Frank, the Nieuwenbergs' granddaughter, Anne Frank, Elly (Bep) Voskuijl, and Esther, an Opekta worker.

both sick, so Edith stayed behind to care for them. Anne was beside herself with happiness. When the wedding party stepped out onto the sidewalk after the ceremony, she jumped up and down with excitement.

To other neighborhood children, the eleven-year-old Anne, Hannah, and Sanne seemed older than the rest of the girls, looking through movie and fashion magazines, collecting photos of movie stars and royalty, and giggling about boys. "They were an inseparable trio, each of them a little more sophisticated than the rest of us—more like teenagers," remembered Eva Geiringer, who lived in the neighborhood.

While Anne's thoughts were quickly turning to boys, she was still a little girl at heart. On Sundays, Otto would often go to the office to catch up on paperwork. Anne and Hannah would sometimes tag along to play, calling from office to office on the telephones, and playing secretary on the typewriter.

A New School and New Friends

In the fall of 1941, Jewish children in the Netherlands were forbidden to go to school with non-Jewish children. Margot and Anne had to leave their schools to attend the Jewish Lyceum (a secondary school). The adjustment to a more traditional, regimented school was particularly hard for Anne, who kept getting into trouble for talking.

Perhaps to help Anne adjust to life in her new school, Otto and Edith agreed to let the family get a pet cat. Moortje, as she was named, quickly became a great favorite of Anne and her friends. Eva Geiringer remembered her visits to their home. "The Franks had a large cat that purred appreciatively when I picked it up. . . . I would wander into the sitting-room to cuddle the cat and find Mr. Frank watching me with amused eyes."

That fall a new member would enter Anne's inner circle. Jacqueline van Maarsen, a new classmate at the Jewish Lyceum, quickly became a close friend. Hannah, who also attended the Lyceum, and Sanne Lederman, who attended a different Jewish school, also remained close to Anne.

Jacque (pronounced "Jackie") and Anne bicycled home together after the first day of school, and she stayed for dinner with the Franks. The two shared a love of movie stars and ancient mythology. They spent countless afternoons doing homework, playing board games, trading postcards and photos of movie stars and royalty, and talking about their latest favorite books.

Anne's Favorite Book Series

Anne Frank and Jacque van Maarsen spent many afternoons reading, talking about, and acting out scenes from their favorite books from a series called Joop ter Heul by Cissy van Marxveldt, a popular Dutch author of young-adult books. The series followed the adventures of Joop and her friends through school, marriage, and motherhood. Anne identified with Joop, who was adventurous and full of personality. In the books, Joop wrote letters to her friends Pop, Pien, Noor, Conny, and her best friend, Kitty.

The cover of one of the Joop ter Heul books by Cissy van Marxveldt is shown here. Anne and Jacque van Maarsen adored the series, often reading or acting out scenes from the books.

Like many Jewish families, the Franks sidestepped the ban on Jews in public theaters by renting projectors and films for special occasions. Edith would provide snacks, and Otto would run the projector. With her flair for the dramatic, Anne would insist on making proper tickets to give to her friends for admission to the "theater."

Anne became fascinated with boys during the school year. She insisted on tagging along with her older sister Margot and her friends, despite Margot's complaints to her mother. She developed a crush on Peter Schiff, who was nearly three years older. He seemed to have found Anne interesting, too, but quickly began ignoring her when his friends teased him about being attracted to a younger girl. She would remember him later as her first love.

Anne became fascinated with boys during the school year.

As the school year progressed and Jews were forbidden to do more and more, Anne, Hannah, Jacque, Sanne, and Ilse Wagner, a friend of Hannah's from her **synagogue**, formed their own ping-pong club. They would hold tournaments on Ilse's dining room table, then adjourn to the Oasis ice-cream parlor, one of the few in the city still open to Jews.

Anne awoke early on June 12, 1942, a school day. It was her thirteenth birthday. As always, her family gave her their gifts on the morning of her birthday. She was particularly excited to receive a red-and-white-checked diary for writing her thoughts about her life.

The diary was really an autograph book used by students for writing poems and gluing in pictures of each other, like a homemade, personalized yearbook. It was perfect for her purposes, though, and she had chosen it herself at Blankevoort's Bookshop on a trip there with her father a few days earlier.

Anne Frank received the red-and-white-checked diary for her thirteenth birthday in June 1942, and took it with her into hiding later that summer.

Her mother baked treats for her classmates, and that afternoon Jacque, Hannah, Sanne, and Ilse gave her their joint gift, a book called *Tales and Legends of the Netherlands*. Her birthday party would have to wait until the weekend, when a larger group of friends would gather for a luscious strawberry tart baked by her mother, party games, and a special showing of *Rin-Tin-Tin and the Lighthouse by the Sea*, a favorite film of Anne's.

A New and Special Friend

In her new diary, Anne could explore thoughts and feelings that she might never have shared with even her closest friends. In fact, she looked upon her diary as another kind of friend. Shortly after receiving it, Anne wrote on June 20, 1942, "I don't want to jot down the facts in this diary the way most people do, but I want the diary to be my friend."

In order to feel as though she were writing to a friend, Anne soon began addressing each entry to a fictional friend named Kitty. Kitty was the name of one of the characters in the Joop ter Heul book series that she and Jacque so loved. The novels, like Anne's own diary, were written as letters from Joop to her many friends. Anne probably did not choose to write to Joop because she identified most with Joop herself.

Prelude to a Disappearance

Despite the family's attempts to keep life as normal as possible, their world was being restricted more and more. Since April 1942, they had been forced to wear a yellow six-pointed star on their outer garments to identify them as Jews whenever they were in public. Those who refused could be imprisoned and fined. Otto Frank felt certain that all the registrations and limitations were hiding a much more sinister plan.

As the school year ended, all outdoor sports were forbidden to Jews, and even bicycles had to be registered. Soon all bicycles owned by Jews had to be turned in to authorities. Virtually all modes of transportation had now been stripped from Jewish citizens. Anne's bicycle had been stolen a few months earlier, but the family decided to hide Margot's instead of registering it, in case of an emergency.

One of the yellow stars, bearing the German word for Jew, which Nazis forced Jews to wear in public.

All the while, Otto and Edith and the office workers at 263 Prinsengracht were secretly preparing for just such an emergency. A few months earlier, Jo Kleiman had suggested to Otto Frank that the upper rooms in the rear building might be an ideal hiding place for the family. The entire office staff, including Miep and Bep Voskuijl, an office worker and daughter of the warehouse manager, pledged to help them remain hidden for as long as it took. Their willingness to risk their lives made the plan possible. At night and on weekends during the spring of 1942, Otto, Jo Kleiman, and Victor Kugler

Workers in Otto Frank's office pose for a photo in 1941. Left to right: Victor Kugler, Esther (last name unknown), Bep Voskuijl, Pine (last name unknown) and Miep Gies.

silently moved furniture, food, and supplies into the rooms in the back of the office building.

Otto and Edith were planning for the family to go into hiding there with the spice expert Hermann van Pels and his wife, Auguste, and son, Peter. Slowly, articles of furniture were disappearing from the Franks' home. When Jacque asked about some missing living room chairs Otto told her that the furniture had been sent out to be reupholstered. Still, the girls were kept in the dark about the plan.

In early 1942, letters were sent to thousands of unmarried Jewish men, telling them to report for work camps. Because married men were at first exempt from the call-ups, marriages among Jews increased dramatically. By May, more than 3,000 Jews had reported to Dutch work camps. By summer, teenaged boys and girls were being ordered to report to work camps as well.

Although the government assured them that the workers, many of whom were unemployed, were living under good conditions, whispers were spreading that the work camps were really death camps where Jews were being killed with poisonous gas.

The horror of the rumors seemed too awful to believe, and those who refused to report for work camp were severely punished. Knowing this, many obeyed the orders, believing that they would be safe. But for many other families who feared the worst, going into hiding seemed the only chance they had to survive until the end of the war. They believed that the Allied forces would quickly overpower the Nazis. Eva Geiringer, whose family went into hiding, remembers, "We thought, 'By Christmas, it will be finished.' And when we went into hiding, we thought *that* would only be for a few months."

Hermann van Pels, c. 1940, worked for Otto Frank as a spice expert. He and his wife, Auguste, and son, Peter, hid with the Franks in the secret annex.

Rushed into Hiding

By the end of June, Anne had a new boyfriend, Helmuth "Hello" Silberberg. He had been sent to Amsterdam to live with his grandparents in 1938 to escape Germany's anti-Jewish laws. A handsome sixteen-year-old, Hello was charmed by the much younger Anne. "She was really very entertaining and extremely lively. . . . I think I was probably in love with her."

On Sunday, July 5, Hello Silberberg had returned home for lunch after visiting Anne and promising to return later. Shortly afterward, the doorbell rang. Edith answered the door expecting to see Hello. Instead, a mailman handed Edith a registered letter commanding Margot to report for work camp the following day. Edith must have felt a sense of panic. In order to protect Margot from reporting, the Franks would have to go into hiding the next

The Final Solution

In January 1942, elite members of the Nazi Party met in a Berlin suburb for the Wannsee Conference to agree on a "final solution" to the "Jewish question." They decided that Europe's Jews would be sent to work camps in eastern Germany and Poland where many would eventually die from the harsh working and living conditions. Others would be killed outright. The first experiments using poisonous gas to kill people had occurred four months earlier. By May 1942, the Nazis had built the first efficient poison-gas chambers at Auschwitz, a concentration camp in Poland.

Despite secrecy about the plan, rumors about what was happening began spreading throughout Germany, Poland, and the Netherlands. The BBC first reported the gassings in June 1942. Many of those who heard the stories refused to believe that even the Nazis could be capable of such an evil plan. Others, like Otto Frank, had no trouble accepting that they could be true.

This photograph shows the inside of a gas chamber at Lublin-Majdanek camp in Poland. Prisoners in Nazi death camps were killed with zyklon B, a poisonous gas, which has stained the walls blue.

day. Edith ran to the Van Pelses' home to warn them that their plans would have to be moved up.

The Van Pelses decided it would be better for them to wait for a few weeks before joining the Franks. They feared that having both families disappear together might raise suspicions about their hiding place.

The girls were told of the plan that day but not where they would be hiding. They were afraid they might say something to betray their plan. When Hello returned to the Franks' house, no one answered the door.

The girls were told of the plan that day but not where they would be hiding.

Miep and Jan came that evening to carry things to their home until they could bring them to the office. The Franks' boarder, Mr. Goldschmidt, unaware of what was going on around him, stopped by to visit with Otto and Edith and stayed until 10:00 p.m. They could not let him in on their secret. They feared that he might betray them, if only by accident.

Miep and Jan made several trips back and forth, hiding as much as they could under baggy coats without looking suspicious. "Everyone was making an effort to seem normal, not to run, not to raise a voice," Miep remembered. "Anne's eyes were like saucers, a mixture of excitement and terrible fright."

Anne's red-and-white-checked diary, the birthday gift she prized above all others, was the first thing she packed in the school bag she brought with her into hiding. She also packed her hair curlers, handkerchiefs, schoolbooks, a comb, and old letters. "Preoccupied by the thought of going into hiding, I stuck the craziest things in the bag, but I'm not sorry, memories mean more to me than dresses."

CHAPTER 4

Vanishing into Thin Air

We both knew that from the moment we'd mounted our bicycles we'd become criminals.

　　　—Miep Gies

Monday, July 6, 1942, dawned with a steady rain. As planned earlier, Miep rode her bike up to the Franks' building at 6:00 a.m. to take Margot to the hiding place. Margot's bike, which had been hidden months before, was waiting outside the front door. Anne, still in her nightgown, stood at the door with her mother and father as Margot got

Margot Frank stands beside her bicycle in this 1938 photo. She would use it for the last time when she rode it into hiding on July 6, 1942.

on her bike. Margot's movements were clumsy, limited by the layers of clothing she wore to take into hiding. The rest of the family would join them later.

Getting to the Hiding Place

Margot removed the yellow star from her coat, and she and Miep rode silently through main streets, looking to anyone who saw them like two young Dutch women heading to work in the rain. They saw no police and no familiar faces as they rode through Amsterdam. Along the way, Miep finally told Margot where she was taking her. "We both knew that from the moment we'd mounted our bicycles we'd become criminals. There we were, a Christian and a Jew without the yellow star, riding on an illegal bicycle," Miep recalled years later. "Margot's face showed no intimidation. She betrayed nothing of what she was feeling inside."

When they reached the empty building, Margot and Miep took their bikes to a storeroom, and Miep led Margot upstairs to the entrance of the secret annex. "Margot was now like someone stunned, in shock. . . . She disappeared behind the door and I took my place in the front office." The warehouse workers, who knew nothing of the plan and had to remain ignorant to protect the secret, would soon be arriving. Everything had to look normal. Miep felt certain that anyone who entered the office at that moment would have heard her heart beating.

As soon as Margot and Miep left, Anne and her parents quickly dressed, each donning extra layers of clothes, and left a note for their boarder, Mr. Goldschmidt, asking him to bring Moortje to a neighbor. Having a cat with them in hiding, Anne's parents reasoned, was simply too risky.

They could not carry suitcases because Jews were forbidden to move from one home to another. They also could not rush and risk bringing attention to themselves as they walked along the streets of Amsterdam. "I was wearing two undershirts, three pairs of underpants, a dress, and over that a skirt, a jacket, raincoat, two pairs of stockings, heavy shoes, a cap, a scarf, and lots more," Anne wrote in her diary. As they walked, Otto and Edith told Anne where they were heading. Nearly an hour later, sweating from the strain and all the clothes they were wearing on a summer morning, they arrived at the office and climbed the stairs to the secret annex that would now be their home.

The family walked through the rooms piled high with clothes, boxes, bags, and old furniture. Margot stood in the disarray looking overwhelmed. Edith, who had so efficiently sorted and organized the night before, was exhausted and unable to think clearly. The two soon lay down on their beds, overwhelmed by the task ahead of them and sadness at the life they had left behind.

They could not carry suitcases because Jews were forbidden to move from one home to another.

Anne and Otto began trying to organize and arrange the piles so that the family could sleep there that night. Among the first duties was to tack simple fabric curtains over the windows so that no one would know people were living there. At night, they covered the windows with blackout panels to ensure that no telltale light glowed from the windows. They had to work silently, as the warehouse staff had no idea that anyone was staying there. Quietly filling cupboards with food and dishes, putting sheets on the beds, and generally tidying up, the Franks transformed what had looked like a storeroom into something resembling a home. By bedtime, they were exhausted and hungry. No one had given a thought to food until nightfall.

Friends Left Behind

While the Franks were adjusting to their new home, friends on Merwede Square were quickly learning that something had happened at the Franks' home overnight. When their lodger, Mr. Goldschmidt, awoke Monday morning, he found meat for Moortje on the kitchen table and the note asking him to take her to a neighbor's. In the trash, Otto also left an address scribbled on a scrap of paper that hinted that they had fled to Switzerland. Soon neighbors were whispering that a German officer, a friend from Otto's days as a soldier in World War I, had helped them escape.

Unaware of what had happened, that afternoon Mrs. Goslar asked Hannah to borrow Mrs. Frank's scales so that she could properly measure the ingredients for strawberry jam. Hannah whistled her usual signal and rang the doorbell so long that she was just about to give up. Then Mr. Goldschmidt came to the door. He told her that the Franks were gone. He let her come in, and he found the scales for her. She was stunned. She ran back home to tell her parents, who were as shaken as she was. Hello Silberberg soon heard the rumors. Having barely escaped from Nazi Germany himself, he did not return to the house or ask any questions. Silence, he believed, was the safest policy.

Later, Hannah and Jacque and Jetteke Frijda, Margot's best friend, returned to the apartment one more time, each hoping for a hidden message from her friend, but it had been too dangerous for Margot and Anne to leave any farewell notes that might have led authorities to them. Jetteke took a book of poetry from Margot's bookshelf, and Hannah and Jacque took Anne's swimming medals as mementos of their friends. Each hoped she would be able to return them at the war's end.

Adjusting to a New Life

While Margot and Edith remained shaken by what had happened, Anne seemed to take things in stride—as much as anyone possibly could. To her lively imagination, it seemed like an adventure. "I don't think I'll ever feel at home in this house," she confessed to her diary, "but that doesn't mean I hate it here. It's more like being on a vacation in some strange **pension**."

Anne's bedroom as it looked when she and her family hid in the secret annex. The photos of movie stars and royalty that she glued to the wall made her feel more at home there.

Anne quickly began trying to make the place feel a bit more like home. Her father had remembered to bring her collections of postcards and photos of movie stars and royalty. She glued them to the walls in the room she shared with Margot. "I was able to plaster the walls with pictures. It looks much more cheerful," Anne wrote in her diary.

During the day when the warehouse workers were in the building, the family had to be virtually silent. Even something as uncontrollable as a cough or a sneeze could have endangered everyone. They would sit quietly in the large room a floor above in what would become the Van Pels family's when they arrived a week later.

During the day when the warehouse workers were in the building, the family had to be virtually silent.

By spending the workday hours in the upper room, they were putting another floor between themselves and the warehouse workers below. No shoes were allowed, and the family did as little walking around as possible. Even flushing a toilet was forbidden. They spent their time reading, playing card games, and later, studying. For the ever-chatty Anne, being silent for hours on end was the hardest task of all.

When one of the helpers would come up in the evening to give them the "all clear" announcement that all the warehousemen had left for the day, the family would stretch, the girls would do some exercises, and they all would head downstairs to Otto's old office to listen to the BBC and Radio Orange.

Days after the Franks had settled into their new home, the Van Pels family joined them in hiding on July 13, 1942. Anne, anxious for company, had looked forward to their arrival. Peter van Pels, their sixteen-year-old son, was an object of particular

Inspiring a Nation

In an age long before television and the Internet, radios offered people their best contact with the outside world.

During World War II, the British Broadcasting Company (BBC) and Radio Orange, the official station of the Netherlands government in exile in London, gave people in countries under German control encouragement and news from the Allied perspective. The BBC gave Radio Orange airtime and studio facilities. Their broadcasts began in July 1940, with an inspiring speech by Queen Wilhelmina telling her fellow citizens that they were waging a battle of good against evil.

Queen Wilhelmina of the Netherlands speaks during a radio broadcast from London to her people under Nazi occupation during World War II. Her messages gave them hope and encouragement.

interest—and disappointment—for Anne. Miep described Peter as "a good looking, stocky boy with thick dark hair, dreamy eyes and a sweet nature." Anne was not so kind in her assessment: "a shy, awkward boy whose company won't amount to much." He did, however, bring his cat, Mouschi, with him, despite having been forbidden to do so. Anne was delighted to have the cat with them.

Life in Hiding

Ordinary people simply don't know what books mean to us, shut up here.

During the early weeks in hiding together, the Franks and Van Pelses quickly found a rhythm to their lives. Up early, long before the warehouse staff arrived at 8:30 a.m., the families took turns using the lavatory, washing up, and folding up beds to give themselves more living space in the daytime.

They marked the passing time by the huge bell tower clock of the Westerkerk (West Church), one of the oldest Protestant churches in the Netherlands. The church was only a few buildings away on the same street. The church's

Westerkerk (West Church), with its bell tower, was located near Otto Frank's offices. Built in 1635, it is one of the oldest Protestant churches in the Netherlands. Its bells rang each quarter hour, marking time for those hiding in the annex.

Westertoren (West Tower) clock bells marked every quarter hour, day and night, with their most elaborate songs playing on the hour.

A Tour of the Hiding Place

The two buildings making up 263 Prinsengracht were joined at each level by halls and stairways. On the ground floor of both buildings was a warehouse for the pectin and spices. The floor above, called the first floor, contained Victor Kugler's office, a storeroom, and a front office, which Miep Gies, Bep Voskuijl, and Jo Kleiman shared. A hallway beside Kugler's office led to the back building, which held Otto Frank's office and a kitchen.

The front of the second floor contained three storerooms for spices and other products. The windows in the back of the third storeroom, which faced the rear building, were painted dark blue to prevent the sun from spoiling the spices. The paint also prevented people from seeing into the hiding place.

The hallway joining the two buildings on this floor led to a plain, gray door to the secret annex. Beyond the door were a small lavatory (a toilet and sink) and two rooms. The larger was shared by Otto and Edith and was used as the family sitting room. The smaller room was Margot and Anne's bedroom and study. Upstairs were a larger room, which was taken by Hermann and Auguste van Pels, and a tiny room where Peter slept. The large room had a gas stove, on which meals for everyone were prepared and eaten. Peter's room also contained a ladder leading up to the attic.

Soon after the families went into hiding, they realized that the plain gray door to the annex was too obvious. Victor Kugler suggested that a bookcase covering the door would make the entrance disappear to any visitors. Kugler asked Johan Voskuijl to

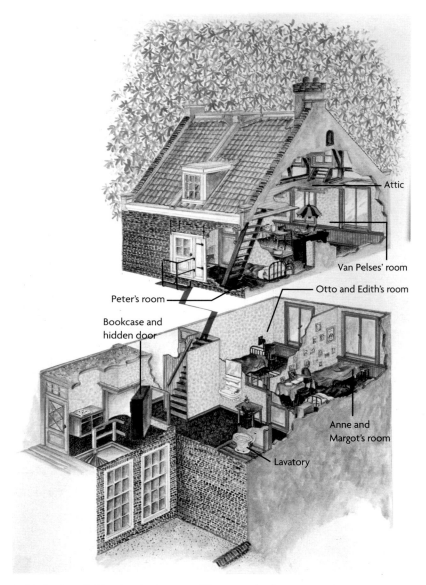

Attic

Van Pelses' room

Otto and Edith's room

Peter's room

Bookcase and hidden door

Anne and Margot's room

Lavatory

In this drawing, a hidden door leads to a small lavatory. Behind it is Anne and Margot's room (right) and their parents' room (left). Upstairs are the Van Pelses' room (rear), where everyone gathered during the day, and Peter's tiny room (front) with a ladder leading to the attic.

This partially opened hinged bookcase hides the entrance to the secret annex where Anne and the others hid. The bookcase was built by Johan Voskuijl, warehouse manager and Bep's father.

build a bookcase. Voskuijl, who managed the warehouse and was the only warehouse worker who knew about the people in hiding, was happy to oblige.

The bookcase was filled with empty account books and looked to all the world like a simple storage space. Cleverly hidden hinges allowed the helpers to enter. Above the bookcase, a framed map of the Grand Duchy of Luxembourg hid the upper edge of the doorframe from prying eyes.

Securing Food

Shortly after Miep Gies arrived at the office each morning, she would slip upstairs to receive a shopping list from Mrs. Frank and Mrs. Van Pels, whisper any news, and promise to return later for a longer visit. Using money the families had saved for their time in hiding and fake food-ration coupon books that Jan had purchased through a **Resistance** organization, Miep and Bep kept the families supplied with food and other necessities.

Modern supermarkets were unheard of in those days, and food supplies were strictly rationed during wartime. Miep would spend a good bit of each morning standing in line at one of the grocery stores nearby, shopping not only for herself and Jan but also for the families in hiding. Jan secured ration books for meat,

The Dutch Resistance

Many people in the Netherlands, and in every other occupied country, were horrified by the actions of the Nazis. A small, brave group refused to stand by quietly. Working in loosely knit organizations, Resistance members labored tirelessly and silently to protect victims and to undermine the German military. In the Netherlands, they largely coordinated efforts to find places for the twenty-five to thirty thousand people who went into hiding during the war.

Risking their lives and safety, Resistance workers made counterfeit money, forged ration cards, published underground newspapers, and distributed food and supplies to those in hiding. Others sabotaged phone and rail lines to interfere with the shipping of Jews and others identified by the Nazis as "undesirables" to death camps.

Members of the Dutch Resistance capture a prisoner of war at the Dutch village of Valkenswaard, near the German border, in September 1944.

Three ration books, such as these, were distributed by the Netherlands government in May 1943. Basic food, clothing, and candy all were rationed.

sugar, flour, and other basics. Miep quickly learned which storeowners were willing to look the other way when she was shopping for so many. Mr. Van Hoeven, whose store sold fresh fruit and vegetables, for example, was involved in a Resistance group and could guess what was going on without anyone telling him. He would regularly haul sacks of potatoes to the office for her, and Peter would carry them up to the annex late at night.

She bought meat from a butcher who was an old friend of Hermann van Pels, and other groceries from a store run by a man involved with the Resistance. Bread was delivered twice a week to the office by a friend of Kleiman who ran several bakeries in the city. The bread, which was officially delivered to the office staff, was shared with the families in the secret annex. When it was affordable, Bep would buy fresh fruit, but as the war dragged on, the high cost and small supply made fruit a rare luxury. She also sneaked a couple of quarts of milk upstairs each day from the supply delivered to the office and often shopped for soap and the other essentials for the families.

In exchange for all the office workers' help, which kept them from finishing their tasks each day, the families would do office work in the evenings. Their efforts helped keep the business running smoothly while the workers helped the families survive. It also gave the families—and especially the young people—a sense of purpose and responsibility.

Passionate Readers

Otto Frank knew from the beginning that spending hours on end in virtual silence would be difficult for Margot and Peter—but especially for Anne. He immediately developed a routine for the three of them. They spent their days studying together or separately. He tutored them in mathematics, geography, history, and literature, and he even gave English lessons. Margot, Peter, and Anne studied or read in their rooms or upstairs in the attic, where they could escape to be alone. They also played board games and cards, read for pleasure, and wrote. By December 1942, Anne had filled her diary, and Bep found her a bound book in which to write. Both Bep and Miep kept Anne supplied with notebooks and ledgers from the office as she filled them with her daily writing. At some point, Margot, too, kept a diary; but it did not survive the war.

Margot threw herself into her studies, excelling as she always had in school. Peter, a boy who liked to work with his hands, was no match for Margot and Anne when it came to school subjects, but he followed the daily schedule and did the best he could. He set up a small workshop in the attic where he could tinker, a pastime that gave him more pleasure than books did.

During her time in hiding, Anne read constantly. She reread her beloved books by Cissy van Marxveldt and many others. She became fascinated with European history, tracing the family trees of Europe's royal families. She also continued to be interested in myths and read the stories of the gods of ancient Greece and Rome.

On Saturdays, Miep would bring them books that Jan had borrowed from Como's, a local bookstore and lending library, and gather up the ones from the previous week. Books were usually read by several people in the annex before being returned, and discussions about them were often passionate. In the evenings, Otto would sometimes read aloud from his favorite German authors; but for his own pleasure, he could often be seen absorbed in a novel by English writer Charles Dickens. Books, which had always been important to the Franks, became a lifeline to the world they once knew. "Ordinary people simply don't know what books mean to us shut up here," Anne wrote in her diary.

By December 1942, Anne had filled her diary, and Bep found her a bound book in which to write.

Nineteenth century British novelist Charles Dickens was Otto Frank's favorite author. Dickens's novels, which Otto read in English, provided Anne's father with moments of escape from his life in hiding.

Visits from the Helpers

Even more important than books to relieve the boredom were visits from the helpers. Anne and the others marked the passage of time by the sound of their footsteps. Miep's early morning trips upstairs to get the shopping lists marked the beginning of the silent portion of the day.

In mid-morning, office manager Victor Kugler might come up to ask Otto Frank a business question and visit for a bit. He would bring the latest newspapers when he could, and once a week, he would bring Anne a copy of the latest movie magazine. He was primarily responsible for running the businesses, and he helped finance the high costs of keeping so many people in hiding by taking money for spice orders without entering them into the accounting books.

Then at midday Bep, the youngest of the helpers, would join them for lunch. She was only ten years older than Anne. Tall and painfully shy, she had joined the company as a typist in 1937, when she was eighteen. After the families went into hiding, Bep quickly became close friends with Anne. She told Anne stories of dating and everyday "girl stuff." Bep, who shared Anne's love of movies, would also relate the stories of the films she had seen. Anne's mother joked that Anne would not have to see any of them after the war because she already knew them by heart.

Even more important than books to relieve the boredom were visits from the helpers.

Jan Gies would come to the office each day to have lunch with Miep. Afterward he would visit while the warehouse workers were out having their own lunch. He would tell them the latest news from the city about the war and bring Hermann van Pels, a heavy smoker, the few cigarettes he could find.

Otto Frank poses with his office staff c. 1935. Left to right: Miep Gies, Johannes Kleiman, Otto Frank, Victor Kugler, and Bep Voskuijl. These staff members were the "helpers" who provided food, supplies, and company for the annex residents.

In the afternoon, Jo Kleiman would visit, sometimes bringing a bit of candy or some other small treat. His cheerful stories, kindness, and his unfailing ability to obtain needed items—or later, as money ran short, to sell items for cash—made his visits a high point of the day.

Later in the afternoon, when things were quiet in the office, Miep would sneak upstairs again to bring them the groceries and stay for a longer visit.

Creating a Friend within Her Diary

If initially Anne's diary gave her an outlet for the things she would have liked to say to her friends, soon it became something more. Her diary became her substitute for the rest of the world. Instead of running down the street to talk to Hannah or Jacque after an argument with her mother, she would turn to her diary and write furiously. It also provided an escape from the frustration of living with other people in such close quarters and a canvas on which to paint word pictures of what she saw there.

Her diary also gave her a place to think deeply about what was happening in the world from which she had been shut away. It was a world she could glimpse only through radio broadcasts, news carried in by the helpers, and her occasional peeks through the slits in curtained windows. Her diary became her lifeline, her confidante, and her dearest friend.

The Van Pelses' room, seen here set up as it would have looked when they were in hiding, served as the group's daytime gathering room and dining room. The constantly drawn curtains kept any prying eyes from seeing inside the annex.

A New Member

The rhythm of life continued into the fall, but beyond the walls of the secret annex, conditions were worsening for Jews in the Netherlands. In November 1942, Miep asked the Franks and Van Pelses if they would consider taking in another person. Her dentist, Fritz Pfeffer, was desperate for a place to escape the constant roundups of Jews taking place that fall. The adults knew him from earlier days, when the Franks would host Jewish friends for get-togethers on Saturday afternoons.

The families discussed the risks involved in taking in another person, and a few days later Otto told Miep that they had decided that, "where seven can eat, eight people can eat as well."

Fritz Pfeffer fled Germany for the Netherlands in 1938. The Jewish dentist joined the Franks and Van Pelses in hiding in November 1942.

Pfeffer moved in with them soon afterward. Sleeping arrangements had to be changed to make room for him. Margot moved into her parents' room, where she slept on a cot. Anne shared her room with Pfeffer. Had Anne's parents realized how difficult their decision would make life for all of them, they might have come up with a different sleeping arrangement.

Pfeffer left behind his fiancée, Charlotte Kaletta, a Christian woman. Nazi laws had forbidden the two to marry. The two were devoted to each other, and being separated was painful for them both.

A proper German gentleman, Pfeffer had little patience for the lively girl who shared his room, and tempers flared nearly from the beginning. Anne's constant outspokenness, questioning, and pleas for attention probably annoyed him greatly.

The feeling was mutual as Anne described him in her diary as "an old-fashioned disciplinarian and preacher of unbearably long sermons on manners." Despite Anne's very negative portrait of him, Miep Gies said he was a kind man. He was the only person not surrounded by loved ones, which must have taken a great toll on him. Nevertheless, Pfeffer and Anne were not the only ones with tempers rising in the crowded secret annex.

Rising Tensions in the Annex

Hermann and Auguste van Pels had known the Franks both through the spice business and through visits to each other's homes, but living together was very different from seeing friends casually. The emotional Van Pelses were very different from the quiet and unfailingly polite Franks. Vicious arguments between the Van Pelses would erupt and end quickly, and then would be followed by affectionate terms of endearment. The Franks found such displays embarrassing at best.

Anne's enthusiasm for the company of the Van Pelses and their son Peter soon changed to annoyance and sometimes to outright anger. To Anne's great irritation, Mrs. Van Pels often commented on the way the Franks were raising her. And when the flirtatious Mrs. Van Pels would turn her attentions to Otto, Anne was furious.

However, Anne seemed to save her sharpest barbs in her diary for Fritz Pfeffer. The two would often squabble about using

Auguste van Pels, shown here before the family went into hiding, often quarreled with Anne's mother about Anne's behavior and housekeeping.

the small writing table in the room. Finding a place to be alone in the crowded quarters was difficult. Anne wanted privacy to write in her diary while Pfeffer wished to read, study Spanish, or write letters to Charlotte, his fiancée. Miep would deliver the letters to Charlotte without telling her where Pfeffer was hiding. Pfeffer wanted to learn Spanish so that he and Charlotte could move to South America after the war.

The two families were not united either. Mrs. Frank and Mrs. Van Pels regularly disagreed about housekeeping, childrearing, and meals. Anne was often the subject of their quarrels. Mrs. Van Pels believed that children should be punished for speaking their minds—and, if necessary, with a smack. Anne's mother would jump to Anne's defense when Anne was criticized by the others for her outspokenness.

Despite Edith's defense of her, Anne was very critical of her mother, whom Anne said treated her as a child and did not understand her. She took offense easily at her mother's remarks and filled her diary with accounts of her mother's shortcomings. When Edith was attentive, Anne thought she was smothering; when she left her alone,

Finding a place to be alone in the crowded quarters was difficult.

Anne called her distant. Without friends to whom she could complain, Anne poured her feelings out to her diary. She wanted to be taken seriously, to be treated as a young woman and not as a girl, but to her mother she was still a child.

Edith seemed to be endlessly patient with her outspoken daughter. She told Otto that such behavior was to be expected of a girl of Anne's age and that eventually Anne would feel differently. In the meantime, she was grateful that Anne felt close to her father.

The Names in the Diary

With the exception of her family, Anne Frank changed the names of most of the people in her diary, because she wanted to hide their identities when she published a book after the war on their ordeal. Here is a key to the real names (used in this book) and the names in the diary:

Real Name	Diary Name
The Hidden:	
Hermann van Pels (spice expert)	Mr. Van Daan
Auguste van Pels (his wife)	Mrs. Van Daan
Peter van Pels (their son)	Peter van Daan
Fritz Pfeffer (dentist)	Mr. Dussel
The Helpers:	
Johannes (Jo) Kleiman (friend and office worker)	Mr. Koophuis
Victor Kugler (office manager)	Mr. Kraler
Bep Voskuijl (typist)	Elli Vossen
Miep Gies (secretary)	Miep van Santen
Jan Gies (her husband)	Henk van Santen
Anne's Friends:	
Hannah Goslar	Lies Goosens
Sanne Lederman	Sanne Houtman
Peter Schiff	Peter Wessel
Hello Silberberg	Harry Goldberg
Jacqueline van Maarsen	Jopie de Waal

Two pages from Anne's diary show a photo of herself. She included many photos in the beginning of her diary.

Celebrations

Food, which was limited at best and very scarce as the war dragged on, was the source of much tension. Anne's sense of fair play was offended by what she saw as selfishness in sharing food. At mealtimes, she complained, Mr. Van Pels "is served first, and takes a generous portion of whatever he likes." She also criticized Pfeffer for his "enormous portions," which left little for the Franks.

Mealtimes were not always grim, though. They also became the focus for celebrations, which the group marked more eagerly than in their previous lives. Birthdays, anniversaries, and especially Jewish holidays were celebrated. The helpers brought little presents for them, and they made gifts for each other.

The kitchen area of the Van Pelses' room included a stove, which was also used to burn trash in the early morning before neighbors would notice the smoke.

Jewish Religious Holidays

The Jewish Sabbath, or holy day of rest, begins at sundown on Friday and ends on Saturday at sundown. It is celebrated with prayer services at a synagogue and with blessings of bread and candles at home before the Friday evening meal. The major religious holidays in the Jewish calendar include Rosh Hashana, the Jewish New Year; Yom Kippur, the day of **atonement**; Hanukkah, the festival of lights; Passover, commemorating the liberation of the Israelites from Egypt; Sukkot, a harvest festival; and Simchat Torah, marking the end of a yearly cycle of readings from the Torah (holy book).

A menorah with the Star of David is shown in this photograph. A new candle is lighted on each evening of Hanukkah, the Jewish festival of lights. Holidays brought those hidden in the secret annex closer together.

These moments helped them not only to mark passing time but also to relieve tensions and help them appreciate that as they stayed together, they remained safe from the clutches of the Nazis. During those moments around the table, reading poems they had written for each other, entertaining themselves with skits and jokes, life seemed normal again, at least for a little while.

CHAPTER 6

Living with Fear

*I heard someone's teeth chattering, no one
said a word . . .*

Learning to live in the secret annex meant living in constant fear of discovery. This fear was always present and it surrounded everything—fear was a blanket that covered their lives and rarely lifted. If the days there were dull, the nights were often terrifying. Huge planes droning overhead in the evening sounded like the thunder that so frightened Anne during her summer vacation with Hannah only a year or two before. Air-raid sirens would punctuate

U.S. Air Force bombers release bombs over Amsterdam's Schiphol airport. Allied bombs completely destroyed it during the war, and stray bombs occasionally landed in the city's neighborhoods during nighttime raids.

the night, sending Anne rushing into her parents' room to be comforted by her father. He would reassure her in his warm, quiet voice and sometimes distract her with the stories of Good Paula and Bad Paula that she had loved as a little girl.

Her fears were real. At times, an Allied bomb meant for a German military target would strike a nearby building, setting it on fire. On one night, buildings a few hundred yards away were burned to the ground. What would they do if their own building were to catch fire? If they could escape the flames by running into the street, they risked being arrested.

Outside the Curtains

The people walking or biking past 263 Prinsengracht during 1942 and 1943 were suffering in their own way from the German occupation of the Netherlands. The helpers were torn between telling the people hidden there what was happening outside on the streets of Amsterdam and sparing them further concern. Should they tell them of the friends and neighbors who had been shipped off in the night? Should they tell them when their own homes were emptied of their prized possessions? "When we had our plate of soup with them at noon, we tried to say nothing about what was happening outside. But it could not be concealed. The air was charged with it. It penetrated through the walls," remembered Jo Kleiman.

If the days there were dull, the nights were often terrifying.

By September 1942, the Netherlands commander for the SS—*Schutzstaffel,* the Nazi terrorist police force—wrote to SS head Heinrich Himmler to proudly inform him that "to date we have marched 20,000 Jews to Auschwitz . . ."

The Fate of Jews in the Netherlands

The fate of Jews in the Netherlands was grim. Approximately one hundred thousand Jews in the Netherlands were sent to death camps during the war. Twenty-five to thirty thousand Jews attempted to go into hiding to avoid this tragic fate. Of those, about eight to ten thousand were caught by German soldiers. Those who had not yet been called to camps and had not slipped into hiding tried to become invisible as they awaited the inevitable knock on the door from the German government. The strain on everyone could be felt in the streets.

"Almost everything happened at night, you know," recalled Jo Kleiman, who helped hide Anne Frank. "We all heard the roar of the cars, the stopping, the pounding on the doors, heard it even in our beds.... There were nights when you had the feeling that in all Amsterdam bells were ringing and fists pounding on doors."

A Jewish family, their yellow Star of David insignia prominently displayed on their coats, leaves their home after being arrested. They will be transported to Nazi concentration camps.

Miep saw the effects of the SS actions as she biked through Amsterdam each day. The Puls Company had been hired by the German government to empty out the homes of Jews and send any valuables to Germany. Nazi supporters and their families then moved in.

"By winter of 1943 it seemed as if all the Jews in Amsterdam were gone," Miep later recalled. "As the Jewish apartments in our quarter were emptied of people, Puls movers would come and empty the homes of possessions and furniture. Quickly a new family would move in. We didn't know who these new families were or where they came from. We did not ask."

As 1942 and 1943 dragged on, the residents of the annex intently followed every newspaper article and radio broadcast. Each encouraging bit of news that the Allies were making progress against the German army was followed by crushing disappointment. Otto moved pins around a map he had hung on a wall of the secret annex to follow the progress of the war. At times, the German army seemed to be outsmarting and overpowering the Allies at every turn.

"By winter of 1943 it seemed as if all the Jews in Amsterdam were gone."

As the war ground on, Miep and Bep had greater difficulty finding food for the residents and themselves. They would stand in line for hours only to find that the food was all gone by the time they reached the front. What food they could scrounge was often rotten. The grocer who had lugged bags of potatoes to the office was swept up in a Nazi raid. Resistance workers who had supplied the illegal ration coupons had been captured. As 1943 ended, coal for heating had become scarce and even electricity was unreliable.

World War II

From the beginning of World War II in 1939 to when peace was declared in 1945, nearly every country in the world became involved. The Axis powers—largely Germany, Italy, and Japan—fought against the Allies—primarily Britain, the Soviet Union, and beginning in 1941, the United States.

The early months of the war did not go well for the Allies. In June 1940, the Battle of Dunkirk, France, led to the evacuation of nearly 340,000 Allied soldiers. France surrendered to Germany later that month. Much of the war in Europe was fought by Allied bombers until 1944, when the Allies landed in Normandy, France, in June. The war in Europe ended in May 1945. The war in the Pacific ended in August of the same year.

World War II would become the largest war in human history, resulting in forty to fifty million deaths of military personnel and civilians.

British and French captives at the Battle of Dunkirk are shown in this May 1940 photograph. Thousands of British soldiers were evacuated and sent home, and Allied armies would not return to the European mainland until 1944.

Otto Frank and Hermann van Pels had planned ahead and stored hundreds of pounds of canned goods, dried beans, and other non-perishables before they went into hiding. Eventually, though, those supplies dwindled. The cost of goods on the illegal **black market** kept rising, and money became scarce in the secret annex. More than a year after their arrival, the Van Pelses reluctantly gave Auguste's beloved fur coat and some jewelry to Miep to sell, to support their family.

Break-ins

As the war continued and supplies across the city dwindled, robberies became commonplace. Thieves were attracted to warehouses in particular, assuming that the warehouses might have supplies of much-needed food or objects that could be sold on the black market. The warehouse at 263 Prinsengracht was no exception. During the time when the families were in hiding, it was broken into four times.

Burglars would look for spices that they could sell. But the intruders, often young men who were anxious to enter and leave as quickly as possible, were not what most frightened the people upstairs. Their fear was that police would be called to the scene and stumble onto their secret. One break-in occurred on the night of March 24, 1943. The culprits were two neighborhood children, Hans and Els Wijnberg, looking for some spices for their mother. As they

Their fear was that police would be called to the scene and stumble onto their secret.

sneaked around downstairs, they heard a toilet flushing. Hans recalled, "That pipe ran through the back of the house just like in our house, so I immediately understood that there were people in the house and I thought: let's get out of here!" The children never told anyone about their adventure until many years later.

Other break-ins were not so harmless. Some robbers stole from the office, including two cashboxes and coupons for 350 pounds of precious sugar. Anne and the rest slept through it all.

The most frightening incident involving a break-in took place in April 1944. The thieves had made a hole in the warehouse door and someone notified the police. Police officers explored the entire building.

Anne described the terror they felt in her diary. "Twice they rattled the cupboard [which hid the door to the secret annex], then a tin can fell down, the footsteps withdrew, we were saved thus far. A shiver seemed to pass from one to the other, I heard someone's teeth chattering, no one said a word, and so we sat until half past 11."

Finding Consolation in Faith

Before her family went into hiding, Anne had paid little attention to her Jewish religion. Edith and Margot went to the synagogue regularly, and Margot had attended religious education classes after school each week. Like her father, Anne rarely attended services at the synagogue and had no interest in learning Hebrew. She joined her family at Hannah's home on Friday evenings for Sabbath meals, but to Anne the occasion was more social than religious.

During the early months in hiding, Anne continued to regard the religious gatherings as social occasions and associated prayer and religion with her mother. "Today I have to read things in the prayer book," she wrote in her

Anne's Chestnut Tree

Anne watched the changing of the seasons through the huge chestnut tree that grew behind the secret annex. It provided a measure of comfort and solace during her years of confinement. Now a symbol of hope, the 150-year-old tree was damaged by an underground oil spill in 1990 and was diagnosed with a deadly fungal infection in 2007. Six saplings grafted from the tree have been raised so that one can replace the tree when it has to be cut down. In 2008, the tree was surrounded by a steel cage to support it, keeping it from falling on surrounding buildings, and in the hope of keeping it alive for a few years longer.

The chestnut tree (right) that inspired hope in Anne Frank was severely diseased by 2007 and became the subject of heated arguments over whether or not to cut it down.

diary in October 1942. "I have no idea why Mummy wants to force me to do that."

In the second year of their confinement in the annex, though, Anne's faith and her Jewish identity deepened. She meditated on what good, if any, could come from their suffering. "Who knows, it might even be our religion from which the world and all peoples learn good, and for that reason and that reason only do we have to suffer now," she wrote in 1944.

Anne's faith was bound closely to her growing affection for the natural world. She saw God in nature. The continuation of the natural cycles—the changing of the seasons, the chirping of birds in the chestnut tree outside the window—gave her solace in the face of the manmade horrors surrounding her. As her understanding of herself grew and matured, so did her faith in God.

After more than a year in hiding, her faith began to offer her relief from fear. In her diary in January 1944, she described a moment in which her fear vanished in the face of the sound of the military planes that had terrified her earlier. "Last night I went downstairs in the dark, all by myself, after having been there with Father a few nights before. I stood at the top of the stairs while German planes flew back and forth, and I knew I was on my own, that I couldn't count on others for support. My fear vanished. I looked up at the sky and trusted in God."

CHAPTER 7

An Author in the Making

When I write I can shake off all my cares. My sorrow disappears, my spirits are revived!

As 1942 spilled into 1943, the tedium of silent days and terrifying nights took its toll on everyone. Anne spent more and more time alone writing. Like many writers, she had a special pen she prized. The fountain pen she so loved had been a gift from Grandmother Hollander when Anne was nine. "My fountain pen was always one of my most prized possessions; I valued it highly, especially because it

Anne Frank posed for this photograph during her last year at the Montessori school, 1940 to 1941. Her memories of her school days fueled her passion for writing in her early weeks in hiding.

had a thick nib, and I can only write neatly with thick nibs," she confided to Kitty.

Holding her pen in a unique way between her index finger and middle finger, she wrote in her room, her parents' room, or at a small desk by the attic window. Everyone knew she kept a diary, but no one was allowed to read it. "She often said, 'Papa, I am writing. Please see that no one disturbs me. I want to write in my diary,'" Otto Frank recalled after the war.

After she filled her original diary, she wrote in notebooks supplied by Miep and Bep and on loose sheets of paper. She kept it all in her father's old leather briefcase.

Expanding into Fiction

In the summer of 1943, more and more Anne began to think of herself as a writer and dreamed of becoming a published author. For months she had been writing extended descriptions of her experiences in hiding. Many of these are included in her published diary. One, called "Villains!" is a lively account of the flea problem that emerged in the rooms. She also wrote about memories of her life before the family went into hiding.

As time went on, though, she began to look to her imagination for inspiration. "A few weeks ago I started to write a story, something that was completely made up and that gave me such pleasure that my pen-children are now piling up," she wrote in her diary in August 1943. She wrote her fictional stories between September 1943 and May 1944. She would often read her short stories aloud to the others, watching their reactions as she read, and then revising until she was happy with the stories. Then she copied them into a large notebook in her best handwriting, rarely crossing out. She included a title page and

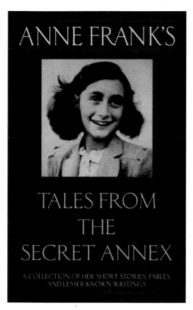

Anne's fiction has been gathered into a single volume called *Anne Frank's Tales from the Secret Annex*. It includes her short stories and *Cady's Life*, her unfinished novel.

table of contents and numbered the pages, as though it were a "real" book.

These short stories, essays, and fables are published as *Anne Frank's Tales from the Secret Annex*. The book also includes sections from a novel titled *Cady's Life* that Anne probably began writing in early 1944. She penned it carefully—obviously after having written at least one earlier draft—in the back of the diary she was keeping in early 1944. She struggled with the story for several months and in the spring wrote in her diary, "Parts of *Cady's Life* are also good, but as a whole it's nothing special."

"Ordinary Documents"

A turning point for Anne's writing career came on March 28, 1944, when Gerrit Bolkestein, the Dutch Minister of Education,

Gerrit Bolkestein, Dutch Minister of Education, Art, and Science, broadcast a plea to citizens to save their wartime writings for future readers. It inspired Anne to prepare her diary for publication.

Art, and Science, broadcast a speech from London. In it, he asked citizens to save their diaries and letters to be put into a center for personal documents of the war. "If our descendants are to fully understand what we as a nation have had to endure and overcome during these years, then what we really need are ordinary documents—a diary, letters from a worker in Germany, a collection of sermons given by a parson or a priest."

Everyone was excited about the possibility of Anne's diary being included. Anne was inspired. A few days later, she began thinking critically about her diary with an eye toward having it published. "When I write I can shake off all my cares. My sorrow disappears, my spirits are revived!" she confided to her diary. However, she questioned her own skill. "I'm my best and sharpest critic. I know what's good and what isn't. . . . But, and that's a big question, will I ever be able to write anything great, will I ever become a journalist or a writer? I hope so, oh, I hope so very much."

In May 1944, she began the task of rewriting the diary for publication. She wrote on sheets of paper that Miep and Bep brought up from the office. She worked feverishly,

In May 1944, she began the task of rewriting the diary for publication.

expanding, combining, and rearranging entries, all with an eye toward a stranger finally reading her beloved diary. She worked through the spring and into the summer on the rewrite of earlier entries while continuing to write her own daily impressions.

She wrote her last entry in her final diary on August 1, 1944. "A bundle of contradictions," was how she began. In it, she talked about the two Annes, the public one, "not accepting other people's opinions, always knowing best, having the last word," and the private one, who "is my own secret."

"I'm afraid that people who know me as I usually am will discover I have another side, a better and finer side. I'm afraid they'll mock me, think I'm ridiculous and sentimental and not take me seriously. I'm used to not being taken seriously, but only the 'lighthearted' Anne is used to it and can put up with it; the 'deeper' Anne is too weak."

In her diary, Anne gives her readers the privilege of knowing both sides of her personality.

Anne's final entry in her final diary is dated August 1, 1944. She and the others were arrested three days later by Gestapo agents responding to an anonymous tip.

Other Wartime Diaries

Anne Frank was not the only young person who kept a diary of her experiences in hiding. Although many were lost, more than fifty-five have survived and been published in the years since Anne Frank's diary first appeared.

Children in the Holocaust and World War II: Their Secret Diaries by Laurel Holliday (Pocket Books, 1995) collects the diaries of more than twenty young people.

Salvaged Pages: Young Writers' Diaries of the Holocaust by Alexandra Zapruder (Yale University Press, 2002) assembles other diaries written by children.

Rutka's Notebook | January-April 1943

Called the "Polish Anne Frank," Rutka Laskier described her life in a Jewish ghetto in Bedzin, Poland, in the diary she kept before her family was shipped to Auschwitz concentration camp in 1943.

CHAPTER 8

Hope Betrayed

I'm longing—really longing—for everything. . . .
I think spring is inside me.

By 1944, during the last months that the people in the
secret annex would remain in hiding, their moods
shifted between hope and despair. Each encouraging
newscast about the Allies seemed to be followed by a bigger
crackdown on people in their city.

Food was becoming extremely scarce, and desperate
people were taking desperate measures—from breaking
into empty warehouses to outright robberies of people in
the street. Nazi crackdowns on Jews and others in hiding
had reached a frenzied pace. Inside the secret annex, the
personalities were grating on each other so much that
sometimes the Franks and Van Pelses simply did not speak
to each other at all.

Despite the boredom and even occasional despair of
those around her, Anne matured both as a writer and as a
young woman during that time. In her first entry of the
year, for example, she looked back on her—sometimes
cruel—treatment of her mother, captured earlier in her
diary, from a very grown-up perspective. Although Anne
knew that she and her mother were very different and
that her harsh judgments about her mother would likely
continue in the pages of her diary, Anne resolved to act
with greater compassion. "The period of tearfully passing
judgment on Mother is over. I've grown wiser. . . .

I [realize] that it's better for unkind words to be down on paper than for Mother to have to carry them around in her heart."

Her new maturity extended to rejoicing in the physical changes she was experiencing with puberty. "I'm carrying around a sweet secret," she confided to Kitty. The physical changes brought a host of emotions and desires. "The sun is shining, the sky is deep blue, there's a magnificent breeze, and I'm longing—really longing—for everything: conversation, freedom, friends, being alone. . . . I think spring is inside me."

Edith Hollander Frank, Anne's devoted mother, suffered her daughter's criticisms and arguments with great patience and love.

First Love

She dreamed of Peter Schiff, her first crush, and soon began to see Peter van Pels, the young man with whom she had shared the secret annex for eighteen months, in a new light. The boy whom she had originally described as "obnoxious" and "a dope," now "gave [her] a wonderful feeling when [she] looked into his dark blue eyes."

She began seeking out Peter to talk, and her feelings seemed to overwhelm her. Over the following months, Anne's budding interest in Peter bloomed. In her diary, she writes lyrically about their quiet

Peter van Pels, who gave Anne her first kiss, was born in Germany in 1926. He and his family fled to the Netherlands in 1937, four years after the Franks settled there.

80

The chestnut tree that Anne saw from the attic window became her link to the natural world. Saplings grafted from it will be planted when it dies.

times together in the attic where they confided their feelings about the world. Anne did most of the talking, it seems. Peter, who was shy by nature and not nearly as bright as Anne, seemed at first content to listen and agree. Soon he was confiding in her, though, and by March, three months before her fifteenth birthday, they shared their first kiss.

During the spring, they spent as much time together as possible, often staring out the attic window at the sky above. "I go to the attic almost every morning to get the stale air out of my lungs. This morning . . . the two of us looked out at the blue sky, the bare Chestnut tree glistening with dew, the seagulls and other birds glistening with silver as they swooped through the air, and we were so moved and entranced that we couldn't speak," she wrote in February 1944.

By May, Otto was concerned about all the time Anne and Peter were spending together. Otto and Anne had a rare argument that ended with both of them in tears over a letter she wrote to her father declaring her independence, saying she needed to be treated with trust as an adult.

Afterward, Anne continued to visit Peter regularly as a gesture of her independence. Soon, though, their ardor began to cool.

Anne, who had idealized Peter through the preceding months, now began to see his flaws. "Peter hasn't enough character yet, not enough willpower, too little courage and strength," she confided to her diary. He remained a sweet boy, her first real love, but she realized that their affection for each other would not survive after the war.

Hope for the War's End

During the spring of 1944, the families in the secret annex clung to news reports about the war. Finally, it seemed that the Allies were making progress against the Nazis. On June 6, they heard that the Allies had landed in Normandy, France. The end of the Nazi terror was in sight. "When I went up to the hiding place, it was as if an electric current were running through the place. Everyone was glued to the radio, waiting for more and more information," recalled Miep Gies.

The landing marked a turning point in the war in Europe. The people in hiding began guessing how long it would take the Allies to reach the Netherlands. They measured it in days. At lunchtime, they all gathered upstairs waiting for American general Dwight Eisenhower, commander of Allied forces, to speak. "He called the day [of the landing] D-Day, and as we wiped tears from our eyes, he assured us that total victory over the Germans would be coming within this very year, 1944," Miep wrote.

"Will this year, 1944, bring us victory?" Anne asked Kitty in her diary that day. "We don't know yet. But it fills us with fresh courage and where there's hope there's life."

As they hoped for quick victory, though, supplies were shrinking throughout the city, and the helpers were hard-pressed to find enough food to support them. In May, the families in the

American soldiers land on the shores of Normandy, France, as part of the D-Day landing in June 1944. Civilians under Nazi occupation hoped that the Allies would quickly liberate them.

secret annex began eating only two meals a day to stretch their supplies. Anne described their main meal one day that month: "Vegetables are still very hard to come by. This afternoon we had rotten boiled lettuce. Ordinary lettuce, spinach and boiled lettuce, that's all there is. Add to that rotten potatoes, and you have a meal fit for a king!"

Despite the sacrifices, Anne remained optimistic that the end was in sight. They celebrated her fifteenth birthday with as much festivity as they could muster. Miep and Bep gathered as many notebooks as they could find for Anne, and Miep scrounged up a few pieces of candy to satisfy Anne's sweet tooth. A day or two earlier, Peter took Miep aside and handed her a few coins, asking her to buy some flowers for Anne. "A few lavender peonies were all that I could find. I gave him the flowers. Red spots rose in his cheeks."

By July, the war situation gave them much hope. The Allies were smashing through German lines throughout Europe. "It seemed that the whole Western Front had been ripped apart and that the German resistance was near collapse," Miep recalled. Tragically, the end did not come soon enough.

. . . supplies were shrinking throughout the city, and the helpers were hard-pressed to find enough food to support them.

Arrest

August 4, 1944, began as an ordinary Friday. Miep stopped by the secret annex early to find out what they needed from the shops. Shortly after eleven, as Miep, Bep, and Jo Kleiman were working in the front office, Miep looked up to see a man standing in the doorway holding a revolver. "Don't move," he said, and then he walked down the hall to Victor Kugler's office.

Kugler heard the noise and opened his door, facing four men, one in a uniform of the Gestapo, the Nazi secret police. Ordered to show them the rest of the building, Kugler showed them the other offices and storage spaces.

"Then we went upstairs and were standing on the landing by the bookcase," Victor Kugler recalled. "My heart was beating very fast. The three Dutch policemen were busy trying to open the bookcase. The moment that I had feared for years had arrived." The officers released the secret catch and pointed their guns at Kugler, ordering him to lead them up the stairs. Edith was sitting in a chair in the room at the top of the stairs, too afraid to move. Margot was crying quietly. Otto Frank was upstairs in Peter's room helping him with an English lesson. At first, he paid no attention to the noise downstairs, but he stood up when he heard the stairs to the upper level squeaking under heavy boots. The door opened and a man with a gun ordered them to put up their hands. He then led them all downstairs to the Franks' room.

Karl Joseph Silberbauer, the Gestapo officer in charge, asked where the valuables were kept. Otto Frank pointed to a closet. "Anne walked back and forth and did not even glance at the briefcase where she kept her diary. Perhaps she had a premonition that all was lost now," Otto wondered later.

Looking around for something in which to store the valuables, Silberbauer grabbed the old briefcase holding Anne's diary entries. "He turned it upside down and shook everything inside it out; there were papers lying all over the wooden floor— notebooks and loose pages," Otto recalled. Then Silberbauer shoved what little of value he had found in the annex into the briefcase and latched it shut.

Like these Jews in Warsaw, Poland, in March 1940, the residents of the annex were taken by Gestapo agents and sent to Nazi concentration camps.

Gestapo officer Karl Joseph Silberbauer, wearing a Nazi swastika pin on his lapel in this photo, led the raid on the secret annex on August 4, 1944.

Silberbauer gave them five minutes to gather their things. As the families grabbed their belongings, he saw Otto Frank's World War I army footlocker in the Franks' bedroom. "Where did you get this?" he demanded.

"It belongs to me," Otto Frank replied. He had kept it since his years as a German officer in World War I.

Silberbauer was shaken to be arresting a German war veteran. "You can take your time," he told him. Otto Frank later wondered whether Silberbauer would have let them go free if the other police officers had not been with him.

Saving the Diary

At 1:00 p.m., a truck pulled up to the entrance of the building. Ten people were led down the stairs: The eight who had been in hiding for more than two years, and two of the helpers, Victor Kugler and Jo Kleiman. Bep had sneaked out of the building earlier. Miep was spared when Silberbauer realized she was a fellow Austrian. She did not see her friends again but heard them being led to the truck.

Around five o'clock, after feeling certain the Nazis were not returning, Jan Gies and Bep entered the building. With Miep, they went upstairs to the secret annex to look around. The rooms had been turned upside down. The contents of drawers and closets were strewn around, and furniture was knocked over. On the floor of the Franks' room, they saw the books and papers they recognized as Anne's diary. They quickly gathered the red-and-white-checked diary, notebooks, and loose papers into their arms and carried them downstairs to the office. Miep put them in one of her desk drawers. "I'll keep everything safe for Anne until she comes back," she said as she closed the drawer.

Who Betrayed Them?

Based on a phone tip received by his boss, Karl Joseph Silberbauer was sent to 263 Prinsengracht in search of Jews hidden there. Who made that call? These are the three suspects who have received the most attention:

William van Maaren was a warehouse manager there in 1943. He had laid traps trying to prove that someone was hidden in the building. The office staff initially suspected him but later discovered that Van Maaren was hiding his own son to avoid military service.

Lena Hartog-van Bladeren had cleaned the offices for a time. She was married to a warehouse worker who joined Frank's company in 1944. Her husband knew that there were Jews hiding in the building. For years, rumors indicated that the caller had been a woman.

Tonny Ahlers, a Nazi Party member, accused Otto Frank in 1941 of criticizing the German war effort, which would have led to severe punishment. At that time, he **blackmailed** Frank into giving him money. Ahlers probably knew where the Franks were hiding and may have reported them to the Gestapo for the reward money.

Learning who made that call may be nearly impossible now. Perhaps someday a researcher will come across records that name the caller, but his or her identity could very well never be known.

CHAPTER 9

From the Annex to the Camps

We are together and we have our peace.

The ten people arrested at 263 Prinsengracht on August 4, 1944, were taken to Gestapo headquarters in Amsterdam, where they were locked in a room together.

"You can't imagine how I feel, Kleiman," Otto Frank said. "To think that you are sitting here among us, that we are to blame."

Anne Frank and her family spent nearly a month in 1944 at the Westerbork Transit Camp. This photograph of the barb-wired grounds was taken in 2004.

Jo Kleiman stopped him before he could finish. "Don't give it another thought," he said. "It was up to me, and I wouldn't have done it differently."

Soon the two helpers would be separated from the other eight. Both survived the war. After only a few days, on August 8, the Franks, Van Pelses, and Pfeffer were put on a passenger train to Westerbork, a transit camp in northeastern Holland. There, Jews waited to be shipped to camps in Poland and Germany, where they worked as slaves or were killed.

It Was Like Freedom

Despite their destination, the captured group was hopeful that the war would end before any tragedy could befall them. After two years of seeing the world only through narrow slits in curtains and a tiny attic window, Anne sat near a window, drinking in the scenery like a desert traveler suddenly given water. "We knew where we were bound, but in spite of that it was almost as if we were once more going traveling, or having an outing, and we were actually cheerful," Otto Frank would recall later.

A few hours later, they arrived at Westerbork. Located on a bleak and isolated swamp, it had grown into a village, supported by the labors of its temporary prisoners. The Franks, Van Pelses, and Pfeffer were all sent to the punishment section, as were all who had gone into hiding. There, they were given blue overalls with telltale red shoulder patches and wooden clogs, a type of foot covering, which fit only by a stroke of luck. Their work was harder and their food rations were smaller (a small bowl of thin soup and a piece of bread) than the other prisoners', but they were with other people for the first time in years, including a few people they had known before.

What Happened to the Captured Helpers?

Within days of their arrest, Johannes Kleiman and Victor Kugler were transferred to Amersfoort, a work camp. A few weeks later, Jo Kleiman developed a bleeding stomach ulcer and was released with help from the International Red Cross. He was sent back to Amsterdam to recover, and two months later, he returned to work.

Amersfoort, shown here c. 1945, was both a transit camp for people awaiting shipment to concentration camps and a work camp for non-Jews like Jo Kleiman and Victor Kugler, who were arrested by the Nazis.

Victor Kugler was transferred from the camp to do manual labor such as digging trenches and clearing roads. In December, he became a translator for a company working for the German army. In early 1945, he was part of a group being marched into Germany for a work detail when British planes fired upon it. In the confusion, he escaped and hid in a nearby farm. He returned secretly to Amsterdam, hidden by local farmers and villagers along the way.

Life in Westerbork

Women and men slept in separate buildings. The day began at 5:00 a.m. with a roll call. They had to line up outside to be counted—rain or shine, summer or winter.

Anne, Margot, and Edith were assigned the dirty and dangerous job of breaking open old airplane batteries and separating the parts, which would be used by the German army. The toxic fumes from the parts made them cough all day. However, they did their work at long tables surrounded by other women and were allowed to talk. The women remembered happier times and shared any gossip about the war.

Despite their situation, Anne seemed happy. She and the others all hoped that the Allies would free the Netherlands before they could be sent to a more dangerous place. They heard that Allied troops had taken Paris on August 25. Surely only weeks remained before the Netherlands would be free, they believed.

American troops march on a street in Paris during the city's liberation in August 1944. Despite the hope of others under Nazi occupation, the war in Europe would not end until May 1945.

Some thought that there would be no more transports to the death camps.

Their hopefulness ended on September 2, 1944, when at morning roll call they learned that a transport train would be departing the following morning. The staff read the names of 1,019 men, women, and children who would be boarding the train in alphabetical order. The Franks and Van Pelses and Fritz Pfeffer were all included. At least, the family thought, they would remain together. They gathered their few possessions into knapsacks and suitcases and agreed that they would meet in Switzerland at Grandma Frank's home after the war if they became separated.

Journey to Death Camps

The next morning, after less than a month at Westerbork, they were roused at dawn and marched to the train tracks where a freight train waited. Seventy-five people were crowded into each cattle car. "The freight cars had been completely sealed, but a plank had been left out here and there, and people put their hands through the gaps and waved as if they were drowning," wrote one observer of a similar transport. Tragically, it was the last train to leave Westerbork for Auschwitz—the most notorious of the Nazi death camps—before the end of the war.

With no windows and a bucket for a toilet, the car quickly began to stink. The cars were so crowded that sitting down was difficult, so some people simply leaned against each other if they were not lucky enough to be near a wall. Occasionally the train would stop for a few minutes or hours and someone would open the door, empty the toilet bucket, throw in a bit of food or water, or demand that the passengers give them valuables. The journey would take three days.

Personal items belonging to prisoners litter the train track leading into Auschwitz concentration camp in Poland c. 1945. More than a million prisoners died there during World War II.

The train reached Auschwitz in Poland on the night of the third day. "The awful transportation—three days locked in a cattle truck—was the last time I saw my family. Each of us tried to be as courageous as possible and not to let our heads drop," Otto Frank recalled years later.

Auschwitz-Birkenau

The doors of the car were pulled open, and the passengers were blinded momentarily by the searchlights and disoriented by the sudden commands yelled at them. "Women to the left! Men to

New prisoners at Auschwitz wait to be transported to the camp. Many of the prisoners were sent immediately to be killed. Others worked as slaves under harsh conditions.

the right!" Children under fifteen and the ill were taken to trucks. They were never seen again.

A doctor quickly looked at each new prisoner, deciding in a moment whether that person would go to the left and be sent immediately to death, or to the right to work. The men who survived this selection were marched to the main camp a few miles away. The women were marched to Birkenau, one of the other camps in the complex. The Franks all survived the selection. They were among only 470 of the 1,019 on the train that night to do so. The rest were sent immediately to gas chambers where they were killed. Their bodies were then burned in **crematoriums** that ran day and night. When a Jew dies, they almost never cremate the body. Thus, the act of cremation was further humiliation for the Jewish people.

Replicas of the furnaces in Crematorium I at Auschwitz, the largest Nazi concentration camp in World War II, are shown in this modern photograph. The original facility cremated seventy thousand bodies of prisoners between 1940 and 1943.

One of those who did not survive for long was Hermann van Pels. A few weeks after arriving, he was selected for gassing. Otto later remembered the day when he and Peter "saw a group of selected men. Among those men was Peter's father. The men marched away. Two hours later a truck came by loaded with their clothing." The gassings that day were among the last to occur at Auschwitz.

At Birkenau, Anne, Margot, Edith, and Auguste van Pels were stripped of their clothes and their heads were shaved. They each received a pair of shoes and a gray saclike dress and were assigned to barracks—buildings used to house the prisoners. Anne, Margot, and Edith remained together. Three-level bunk beds with thin straw mattresses lined the room. Each person was given a metal bowl, an enamel cup, and a spoon. Some were lucky enough to have a knife. If a prisoner lost her bowl, she had no way to eat the dark liquid that passed for food.

Making a Life in Hell

Whistles blew to wake up the inmates at 3:30 a.m. each day. Roll call required them to line up in groups of five rows of five to be counted. The counting could last for hours, even in the winter cold. If the numbers did not match the records or if someone was missing, it would start over again. The routine kept track of any missing prisoners, but more importantly, it made the internees feel less than human. Anne's anger with her mother that flowed through her diary was gone. She and her mother and sister were inseparable, relying on each other for the strength they needed to survive.

Breakfast was a ladleful of brown liquid "coffee" and a piece of bread. "We got a [small] loaf . . . for six of us," Janny Brandes-Brilleslijper, who was there with Anne, recalled, "which meant that each of us would get a one-inch piece of bread." She and her sister shared a knife. "We sliced that one-inch strip of bread into thin slices so that we would have more tiny strips that would last longer."

The routine kept track of any missing prisoners . . . [and] made the internees feel less than human.

Otto, Peter, and Fritz Pfeffer survived similarly in the men's camp. Sal de Liema, a fellow prisoner, remembered, "The biggest problem was to save your brain. Don't think about every day. We talked about **Beethoven** and **Schubert** and opera. We would even sing, but we would not talk about food." Hunger was a constant in their lives. Inmates worked at backbreaking tasks fueled by only a few hundred calories each day.

In October, two selections affected the former residents of 263 Prinsengracht. On October 29, Fritz Pfeffer was sent to a camp in Germany, where he died in late December. The next day, a selection at the women's camp sent Anne and Margot to the Bergen-Belsen concentration camp in Germany. The girls had been living in an isolation barracks because they both had scabies, a skin infection caused by lice. On the day of the selection, Rosa de Winter, a fellow inmate, remembered Anne and Margot "approaching the selection table with the SS men . . . Anne

Prisoners struggle to survive near the dead and dying at Bergen-Belsen camp in 1945. Conditions there were among the worst of any Nazi camp by the end of the war.

encouraged Margot, and Margot walked erect into the light." The girls were identified as "ill but potentially capable of recovering" and joined about 8,000 women on the long train ride to Bergen-Belsen.

Edith, who was left behind at Auschwitz, was distraught—not for herself but for her daughters. Afterward, Edith's physical and mental health declined quickly, and she died in January 1945.

Bergen-Belsen

Without their mother or father to protect them, Margot and Anne boarded a cold, damp cattle car with some bread, cheese, margarine, and water. Five days later, they arrived at Bergen-Belsen and were forced to march another four miles to their destination: a tent camp that had been quickly built to house thousands of new inmates being shipped from other camps as the Allies were closing in. The huge cloth tents were erected on the cold ground with no floors and no beds.

After a terrible storm swept through, pulling many tents up from the ground, including Anne and Margot's, the girls were moved to a barracks where three-level bunks at least got them off the ground. Food and water were scarce, but the girls were able to walk around during the day. Anne was particularly attracted to the fence made of bales of straw

Without their mother or father to protect them, Margot and Anne boarded a cold, damp cattle car . . .

wrapped with barbed wire. It separated her section of the camp from the area that housed "exchange prisoners"—inmates who had been selected for better treatment so that they could be exchanged with the Allies for German prisoners of war.

Bergen-Belsen camp was designed to house ten thousand, but there were sixty thousand prisoners in 1945. Many were housed in tents, in which prisoners slept on the ground.

One day in November, Anne met Nanette Blitz, a friend from the Jewish Lyceum in Amsterdam. Nanny, as Anne called her, told her about her friends, and she and Anne reminisced about their life at home. Anne told her about her time in hiding and confided that she planned to write a book based on her diary after the war. Her parents, she told Nanny, were almost certainly dead. She assumed that her mother, who was left behind, was killed in Auschwitz. She also believed that her father would have been seen as an old man by the Nazis and sent to the gas chambers.

. . . she and Anne reminisced about their life at home.

At the end of that month, Auguste van Pels arrived in Bergen-Belsen and quickly became part of a small support group of which

Prisoner Exchange Program

In 1943, Nazis set up a special camp for Jewish prisoners who could be exchanged for German prisoners of war being held by the Allies. These Jewish prisoners were treated better than the rest of the internees in the camps. They received regular packages from family and international aid organizations and were given larger food rations. The Nazis wanted them to be able to say that they had been treated well in the camps to hide the truth about the living conditions and treatment endured by millions of other prisoners.

Anne and Margot were part. "We watched each other like hawks for any signs of giving up. . . . We saw each other getting thinner and thinner, and shared whatever food we could get hold of," recalled one member who survived the war. Their daily rations had by then been cut to a bowl of turnips cooked in water and a slice of bread.

Reunion with Hannah Goslar

Hannah Goslar, Anne's friend since their Montessori kindergarten days, had been living in Bergen-Belsen, on the other side of the straw-and-barbed-wire fence, for about a year. She and her father and sister Gabi were on a list of Jewish families waiting to immigrate to **Palestine** as part of the prisoner exchange program. Hannah's mother, Ruth, had died in childbirth while Anne and her family were in hiding. As an exchange prisoner, Hannah had been relatively well cared for.

One day, Auguste van Pels heard that Hannah was at the camp. She returned to the barracks and told Anne the news. Anne quickly returned to the fence calling Hannah's name. They spoke only briefly because the guards forbade prisoners to speak to each other across the fence. The fence was too solid and too tall for them to see each other. "So we stood there, two young girls, and we cried," Hannah recalled. They told each other about what had happened to them in the two years since they had been together. Anne told Hannah that they had almost nothing to eat on her side of the fence and were very cold. Hannah, as an exchange prisoner, had more to eat and had been allowed to keep her clothes.

Anne told Hannah that they had almost nothing to eat on her side of the fence and were very cold.

They arranged to meet again the next night. Hannah packed a bundle with a wool jacket, some biscuits, sugar, and a tin of sardines. She threw it over the tall fence, but another woman caught it and ran away with it. The next evening, she gathered together another bundle and threw it to Anne. This time Anne caught it.

When Hannah returned to the fence a few nights later, she learned that Anne's section of the camp had been moved. They never saw each other again.

"We Have Our Peace"

In February, Auguste van Pels was transferred to Buchenwald camp in Germany and then again in April to Theresienstadt, a camp in the current Czech Republic. She died in April or early May 1945.

Both Margot and Anne became very sick with typhus, an infection caused by the bites of lice. They were transferred to a quarantine barracks. Lientje and Janny Brilleslijper were working as nurses among their fellow inmates. They visited the girls in quarantine. "At least it was warm there and there were only two of them in the bunk," Lientje remembered. "Anne said, 'We are together and we have our peace.' Margot said scarcely

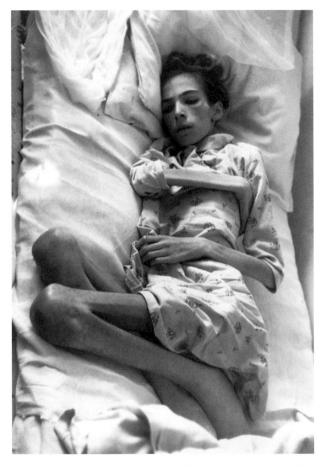

Like Anne and her sister, Margot, starvation and disease ravaged the body of concentration camp prisoner Vera Berger, who was found by Allied soldiers while liberating Bergen-Belsen in 1945.

A liberated Bergen-Belsen prisoner receives a dusting of insecticide from a British soldier in May 1945. The treatment was done to kill the insects carrying deadly typhus.

anything. She had a high fever and smiled contentedly. Her mind was already wandering."

Margot died some time in March. Anne died a few days later. Their friends carried their bodies to a pit that had been dug as a common grave nearby. On April 15, 1944, only a few weeks after their deaths, British troops liberated the camp.

The Holocaust

Holocaust is the term used to describe the ordered killing of millions of Jews by the Nazis during World War II. It comes from a Greek word meaning, "to sacrifice by fire." Although exact numbers are not available, scholars estimate that the Nazis murdered some six million Jews as part of their "final solution" to the "Jewish problem." They wished to exterminate all Jews and others whom they believed were racially inferior to Germans.

The Roma, or gypsies, were another ethnic group singled out by the Nazis for **annihilation**. Like the Jews, they were gassed in death camps. Some five hundred thousand died in camps during the war.

Great numbers of Poles, Russians, Jehovah's Witnesses, Communists, homosexuals, and physically and mentally handicapped adults and children were also killed by the Nazis. Today, there are many museums in the United States and around the world that keep the memory of Holocaust victims alive.

Shoes once belonging to death-camp victims are piled in a heartbreaking display at the U.S. Holocaust Memorial Museum in Washington, D.C.

CHAPTER 10

The Aftermath

I want to go on living even after my death!

Otto Frank remained in Auschwitz until the end of the war in Europe. Through the fall of 1944, he worked on a road-building crew until the hard labor, starvation, and cruel treatment left him near death. A fellow prisoner who was a doctor took pity on him in November and allowed him to stay in the sick barracks. Although there was no medical treatment, he did not have to do hard labor. The doctor's kindness kept him alive.

Peter van Pels, who was fortunate enough to get a job in the camp post office, cared for Otto as a son would have cared for his father. He found extra rations for him and visited him regularly. In mid-January 1945, the Nazis abandoned the camp when they learned that Allied forces were approaching. All the inmates who were able to walk were being forced to evacuate. Otto begged Peter to hide in the infirmary and await the Allied liberators, who would soon arrive.

Peter instead left camp with thousands of other prisoners on foot for Wodzislaw Slaski, Poland, with only their thin camp clothes to wear and no food to eat. There, a train carried them to Mauthausen, a slave labor camp in Austria. He died at that camp in May 1945, just before Allied troops entered it.

Otto was one of the sick and dying prisoners that Soviet soldiers found when they liberated Auschwitz on

As the Allies approached Auschwitz, Peter van Pels was evacuated to Mauthausen, where he died just before the camp was liberated. This photo shows starving prisoners in their barracks at Mauthausen camp, celebrating their liberation by U.S. troops on May 5, 1945.

January 27, 1945, as part of their push across Poland from the east. The soldiers opened up the Nazis' supply rooms, which held plenty of food, to feed the starving inmates. After a few weeks at the camp in Soviet care, Otto began his return to Amsterdam in the hope that he would find his wife and daughters.

Along the way in his months-long journey, he met Rosa de Winter, who told him that she had been with Edith when she died. He returned to Amsterdam in June 1945, and went to Miep and Jan Gies's apartment, still hopeful that he would find his daughters.

He soon returned to the office, but spent most of his time and effort searching for news of Margot and Anne. Each day he would visit public buildings where bulletin boards held names of the missing. On one trip to a Red Cross station, he found Anne and Margot's names on a list of those who had died in the camps. He learned from a Red Cross worker that Janny Brilleslijper had given the information, and he went to speak to her. He knocked on her

Weakened prisoners are escorted out of the gate of Auschwitz at the liberation of the camp by Soviet soldiers in 1945. The words above the gate read *Work Brings Freedom*.

door and asked about his daughters. When she told him that she had been with them when they died, he fell into a chair, nearly fainting from shock and grief.

"It Was a Revelation"

He returned to Miep and Jan to share the news. At the news of Anne's death, Miep Gies gave Otto Frank all the papers she had saved to return to Anne. Weeks would pass before he could bear to begin reading them. When he did, he wrote later, "I began to read slowly, only a few pages each day, more would have been impossible, as I was overwhelmed by painful memories. For me,

Anne Frank's first diary entry is shown here. Anne's insights and writing in it surprised Otto and his family and friends, who urged him to publish it.

it was a revelation. There, was revealed a completely different Anne to the child that I had lost. I had no idea of the depths of her thoughts and feelings."

In the fall of 1945, Otto began translating excerpts from the diary into German to share with his family in Switzerland, most of whom did not speak Dutch. The family members were amazed by the power of Anne's writing.

Working from Anne's first and revised versions of the diary, and incorporating several of the tales she wrote about events that occurred in the secret annex, Otto carefully typed a new version. At first, Miep refused to read it, believing that the memories it would stir would be too painful. He began sharing it with other friends, including friends of Anne's who survived the war. Not all of them

The family members were amazed by the power of Anne's writing.

thought he should publish it. They believed that it had been her private diary, which she let no one read during her lifetime. Yet, Otto knew that Anne had planned to publish something based on it after the war, and he knew its power.

At first, publishers in the Netherlands and Germany turned it down. Then, in 1946, he sent the manuscript to a friend who worked in publishing. Through the friend, it reached historian Jan Romein, who wrote a piece praising it in *Het Parool*, a Dutch newspaper, in April.

Soon publishers were clamoring for the manuscript. It was published as *The House Behind* by Contact, a Dutch publisher, in March 1947. German and French editions followed in 1950, and an American edition, titled *Anne Frank: The Diary of a Young Girl*, was published in 1952. A stellar review in the *New York Times* led to sales of forty-five thousand copies within a week.

The book became a bestseller again a few years later when the story was adapted into a play, called *The Diary of Anne Frank*, which opened in 1955. The screenplay won a Pulitzer Prize, the most prestigious literary award in America. In 1959, it was made into a movie of the same name and won three Academy Awards.

Saving 263 Prinsengracht

In 1956, the building that had housed Otto Frank's businesses and hidden his family, the Van Pelses, and Pfeffer for more than two years was scheduled to be demolished. Otto and others established an organization to preserve it and turn it into a museum to spread Anne's message of religious and ethnic tolerance.

The building reopened as the Anne Frank House in 1960. In the 1970s, it was renovated, and in 1999, the front building was expanded into a visitors' center. Today nearly one million people from all over the world visit the Anne Frank House each year. The museum also creates traveling exhibits and offers lesson plans for teachers to use in their classrooms.

The Anne Frank House, a museum dedicated to her memory and to reminding visitors of the terrible toll of prejudice, stands where Anne and the others hid during World War II.

In 2006, the Anne Frank House created a virtual Anne Frank Tree on the Internet. In the background, visitors can hear birds in the tree, and every few minutes, the sound of the bells from the Westerkerk tower that Anne heard each day while hidden in the secret annex. The tree lets visitors enter their names on virtual leaves and to write about what Anne's words on freedom, caring, and courage mean to them personally.

Otto Frank's Life after the War

During Otto Frank's return to Amsterdam after the war, he met Eva Geiringer, who had been at school with Anne. She introduced him to her mother, Fritzi, whose husband had been killed in the camps. Over time, Otto and Fritzi became friends, and in 1953, they married.

In 1963, Otto and Fritzi set up the Anne Frank Foundation in Basel, Switzerland, where they had moved. The foundation is a charitable organization that uses the proceeds of the royalties from the diary and Anne's other writings to support educational causes.

In an interview years after the war, Otto Frank was asked what lessons he had learned from his experience in World War II. He said, "We cannot change what happened anymore. The only thing we can do is to learn from the past and to realize what discrimination and persecution of innocent people means. I believe it's everyone's responsibility to fight prejudice."

Otto spent the rest of his life traveling the world spreading Anne's message. He died in 1980 at the age of ninety-one.

Otto Frank speaks with students at the laying of the cornerstone of the Anne Frank School in Wuppertal, Germany, in 1959. More than 200 schools around the world bear her name.

Anne Frank's Legacy

Anne Frank's diary is said to be the most popular work of nonfiction in the world after the Bible. Each year it is read by students in schools everywhere and reread by adults who remember it as the book that gave a human face to the tragic story of the Holocaust. More than thirty million copies of the book have been published in sixty-five languages.

"I want to go on living even after my death! And that's why I'm so grateful to God for having given me this gift, which I can use to develop myself and to express all that's inside me," Anne wrote. Her wish to survive beyond her death has been realized far beyond what she could have imagined while hidden inside the secret annex, peeking through curtained windows at the sky.

Covers of Anne Frank's diary published in many translations are displayed on a wall. More than 30 million copies of the diary have been published in 65 languages.

CHAPTER 11

What Happened to the Others?

I believe it's everyone's responsibility to fight prejudice.

—Otto Frank

All of the people who loved and helped Anne Frank and her family during those turbulent times had their own stories of courage and sacrifice that cannot be told in this book. Below are brief summaries of what happened to Anne's family and friends during the war and the years after.

FRANK, ALICE STERN—Anne's grandmother survived World War II in Basel, Switzerland. She died in 1953.

GEIRINGER, FRITZI—After her marriage to Otto Frank in 1953, Fritzi and Otto settled in Switzerland near Otto's family. For years, she helped Otto answer the letters written to him from the world over. She died in 1998.

GIES, MIEP AND JAN—Miep and Jan Gies remained in Amsterdam after the war. In 1950, Miep gave birth to a son and quit her job to care for her family. Jan died in 1993. In 1996, Miep and filmmaker Jon Blair accepted an Academy Award for best documentary for *Anne Frank Remembered.* She continues to live in Amsterdam.

Miep and Jan Gies in 1987, when they were honored in New York with the Anti-Defamation League's Courage to Care Award for sheltering Anne Frank and the others from Nazi persecution.

GOSLAR, HANNAH—Anne Frank's childhood friend survived her time in Bergen-Belsen. In 1947, she emigrated to Jerusalem where she became a nurse. She married and had three children and ten grandchildren. She lives in Jerusalem.

HOLLANDER, JULIUS AND WALTER—Anne Frank's uncles became U.S. citizens and lived in Massachusetts. In 1963, they moved to New York where Julius died in 1967, and Walter died in 1968.

KLEIMAN, JO (JOHANNES)—Otto Frank's old friend and one of the helpers, ran Opekta when he returned from the Amersfoort work camp. He took charge of the company completely when Otto Frank moved to Switzerland in 1952. He died in his office in 1959.

KUGLER, VICTOR—Helper and office manager, Victor Kugler returned to Amsterdam after escaping from his German captors in 1945. He emigrated to Toronto, Canada, in 1955. He died there in 1981.

LEDERMAN, SANNE—One of Anne Frank's oldest friends, Sanne Lederman spent four months at the Westerbork transit camp in 1943. She and her parents were killed in Auschwitz in November of that year.

SCHIFF, PETER—Anne Frank's first romantic crush,
Peter Schiff was arrested in 1943, and sent to the
Westerbork transit camp, then transferred to Bergen-
Belsen and finally to Auschwitz, where he died.

SILBERBERG, HELLO (HELMUTH)—One of Anne Frank's
young boyfriends, Hello escaped from Amsterdam to
Brussels, Belgium, in 1942, where his parents were
living. Soon conditions worsened there, and they
too went into hiding. He and his family survived
the war. He and his parents emigrated to the United
States after the war. He married a woman he met in
Brussels and lives in New Jersey.

VAN MAARSEN, JACQUE (JACQUELINE)—Anne Frank's
childhood friend survived the war because her
mother, a Christian, was able to convince the
authorities that Jacque and her sister were Christians.
After the war, she finished school and married a
childhood friend. She wrote *My Friend Anne Frank* in
1990. She and her husband have three children and
live in Amsterdam.

VOSKUIJL, BEP—Helper Bep Voskuijl left Opekta after
the war. Her father, Johannes, who was warehouse
foreman and built the bookcase
that hid the door to the secret
annex, died in 1945. Bep
married in 1946 and remained
in Amsterdam, where she died
in 1983.

Jacqueline van Maarsen is pictured here in 2007 at the
Edinburgh International Book Festival. She spoke there
about her book about her childhood friend Anne Frank.

Glossary

annihilation—to be killed or destroyed.

anti-Semitism—hostility or prejudice against Jews as a religious, ethnic, or racial group.

atonement—reconciliation with God through sacrifice.

Beethoven, Ludwig van—German classical composer.

black market—illegal trade in goods.

blackmailed—took money to keep quiet about an incident in another person's past.

Brown Shirts—members of a private Nazi army known for its violence and brutality. Also called Storm Troopers.

chancellor—chief of state.

concentration camps—camps in which political prisoners or prisoners of war are confined. Many Nazi concentration camps were set up to kill their prisoners systematically.

crematoriums—large ovens for burning dead bodies.

dictator—an absolute ruler who usually punishes anyone who stands in his or her way.

emigrated—having left one's country to live in another country.

hooligans—hoodlums; people who commit violent acts.

Nazis—members of the National Socialist German Worker's Party in Germany, which controlled the country from 1933 to 1945.

Palestine—area of the Middle East now made up of Israel and the West Bank.

pension—a hotel or boardinghouse in Europe.

rabble-rousing—stirring up crowds of people to hatred or violence.

Resistance—an organization within a conquered country engaging in sabotage and secret operations against the occupying forces.

Sabbath—weekly day of rest and worship for a religious group.

Schubert, Franz—Austrian classical composer.

streetcar—a public vehicle on rails that carries passengers through city streets.

sympathizer—a supporter of a belief.

synagogue—a house of worship for a Jewish congregation.

visas—attachments to a passport giving the holder the right to enter a country.

Bibliography

Books

Anne Frank House. *Anne Frank House: A Museum with a Story.* Amsterdam: Anne Frank Stichting, 2001.

Anne Frank House. *Inside Anne Frank's House: An Illustrated Journey through Anne's World.* New York: Overlook Duckworth, 2004.

Foot, Michael Richard Daniell. *Holland at War Against Hitler.* London: Routledge, 1990.

Frank, Anne. *The Diary of a Young Girl: The Definitive Edition.* New York: Bantam, 1997.

Frank, Anne. *Anne Frank's Tales from the Secret Annex.* New York: Bantam, 2003.

Gies, Miep with Alison Leslie Gold. *Anne Frank Remembered: The Story of the Woman Who Helped to Hide the Frank Family.* New York: Simon and Schuster, 1988.

Gold, Alison Leslie. *Memories of Anne Frank: Reflections of a Childhood Friend.* Scholastic, 1997.

Laskier, Rutka. *Rutka's Notebook: A Voice from the Holocaust.* New York: Time, 2008.

Lee, Carol Ann. *The Hidden Life of Otto Frank.* New York: HarperCollins, 2003.

Lee, Carol Ann. *Roses from the Earth: The Biography of Anne Frank.* London: Penguin, 2000.

Lindwer, Willy. *The Last Seven Months of Anne Frank.* New York: Anchor Books, 1992.

Muller, Melissa. *Anne Frank: The Biography.* New York: Henry Holt, 1998.

Netherlands Institute for War Documentation. *The Diary of Anne Frank: The Revised Critical Edition.* New York: Doubleday, 2003.

Pressler, Mirjam. *Anne Frank: A Hidden Life.* New York: Puffin/Penguin, 2001.

Schnabel, Ernst. *The Footsteps of Anne Frank.* London: Pan Books, 1961.

Van der Rol, Ruud and Rian Verhoeven. *Anne Frank: Beyond the Diary.* New York: Puffin/Penguin, 1995.

Van Maarsen, Jacqueline. *My Friend Anne Frank.* New York: Vantage Press, 1996.

Zapruder, Alexandra. *Salvaged Pages: Young Writers Diaries of the Holocaust.* New Haven: Yale Nota Bene, 2004.

Articles

Stam, Dineke. " 'I Was the Burglar:' Hans Wijnberg: 'I Discovered that People Were Hiding There.' " *Anne Frank Magazine* 1999.

Web Sites

Anne Frank House. http://www.annefrank.org

Anne Frank Tree. http://www.annefranktree.com

Encyclopedia Britannica, 2008. Encyclopedia Britannica Online. http://www.britannica.com

Montessori: The International Montessori Index. http://www.montessori.edu

U.S. Holocaust Memorial Museum. http://www.ushmm.org

Source Notes

The following list identifies the sources of the quoted material found in this book. The first and last few words of each quotation are cited, followed by the source. Complete information on each source can be found in the Bibliography.

Abbreviations:

AF—*The Diary of a Young Girl: The Definitive Edition*

AFH—*Anne Frank House: A Museum with a Story*

AFR—*Anne Frank Remembered: The Story of the Woman Who Helped to Hide the Frank Family.*

BIO—*Anne Frank: The Biography*

BUR—"'I Was the Burglar:' Hans Wijnberg: 'I Discovered that People Were Hiding There,'" *Anne Frank Magazine*

FAF—*The Footsteps of Anne Frank*
HL—*Anne Frank: A Hidden Life*
LSM—*The Last Seven Months of Anne Frank*
OF—*The Hidden Life of Otto Frank*
RCE—*The Diary of Anne Frank: The Revised Critical Edition*
RFE—*Roses from the Earth: The Biography of Anne Frank*

INTRODUCTION: Anne's Prized Gift
PAGE 1 *"I still believe . . . good at heart . . ."*: AF, p. 328
PAGE 1 *"It's a wonder . . . return once more."*: AF, p. 328

CHAPTER 1: Born in the Shadow of War
PAGE 2 *"a little rebel . . . her own."*: OF, p. 31
PAGE 4 *"a little rebel . . . at night."*: OF, p. 31
PAGE 4 *"many times . . . nursery songs."*: OF, p. 31
PAGE 11 *"She peeks . . . a walk,"*: FAF, p. 25
PAGE 11 *"Won't someone . . . lady?"*: BIO, p. 49

CHAPTER 2: A New Life in Amsterdam
PAGE 12 *"When she played . . . the others."*: FAF, p. 43
PAGE 14 *"Here come Anna, Sanne, and Hannah,"*: BIO, p. 52
PAGE 15 *"She always . . . tumbled over,"*: FAF, p. 33
PAGE 18 *"She was rather small . . . the others."*: FAF, p. 43
PAGE 19 *"When he . . . shine,"*: LSM, p. 13
PAGE 21 *"My husband . . . and harder."*: RFE, p. 51
PAGE 22 *"there was nothing . . . any spice."*: AFR, p. 47

CHAPTER 3: Making the Most of Difficult Times
PAGE 25 *"Memories . . . dresses."*: AF, p. 20
PAGE 28 *"I don't know . . . be worried."*: RFE, p. 52
PAGE 30 *"We don't have . . . how it is."*: RFE, p. 71
PAGE 30 *"We sleep . . . disturb us."*: BIO, p. 125
PAGE 31 *"They were . . . like teenagers,"*: RFE, p. 59
PAGE 31 *"The Franks had . . . amused eyes."*: RFE, pp. 58–59
PAGE 34 *"I don't want . . . my friend."*: AF, p. 7
PAGE 37 *"We thought, . . . few months."*: RFE, p. 93
PAGE 37 *"She was . . . love with her."*: RFE, p. 100
PAGE 39 *"Everyone was . . . terrible fright."*: AFR, p. 95
PAGE 39 *"Preoccupied by . . . dresses."*: AF, p. 20

CHAPTER 4: Vanishing into Thin Air
PAGE 40 *"We both knew . . . become criminals"*: AFR, p. 96
PAGE 41 *"We both knew . . . feeling inside."*: AFR, p. 96
PAGE 41 *"Margot was now . . . front office."*: AFR, p. 97

PAGE 42 *"I was wearing . . . lots more,"*: AF, p. 20
PAGE 44 *"I don't think . . . strange pension."*: AF, p. 26
PAGE 45 *"I was able to . . . more cheerful,"*: AF, p. 26
PAGE 46 *"a good looking, . . . sweet nature."*: AFR, p. 107
PAGE 46 *"a shy, awkward, . . . amount to much."*: AF, p. 30

CHAPTER 5: Life in Hiding
PAGE 47 *"Ordinary people . . . shut up here,"*: BIO, p. 194
PAGE 54 *"Ordinary people . . . shut up here,"*: BIO, p. 194
PAGE 58 *"where seven . . . as well."*: AFR, p. 133
PAGE 59 *"an old-fashioned . . . on manners."*: AF, p. 70
PAGE 62 *"is served . . . he likes."*: AF, p. 121
PAGE 62 *"enormous portions"*: AF, p. 123

CHAPTER 6: Living with Fear
PAGE 64 *"I heard . . . a word"*: BUR, p. 35
PAGE 65 *"When we had . . . the walls,"*: FAF, p. 97
PAGE 65 *"to date . . . Auschwitz . . ."*: HL, p. 125
PAGE 66 *"Almost everything . . . on doors."*: FAF, p. 97
PAGE 67 *"By winter . . . not ask."*: AFR, p. 167
PAGE 69 *"That pipe ran . . . out of here!"*: BUR, p. 33
PAGE 70 *"Twice they rattled . . . past 11."*: BUR, p. 35
PAGES 70/72 *"Today I have . . . do that."*: BIO, p. 238
PAGE 72 *"Who knows, . . . suffer now."*: BIO, p. 239
PAGE 72 *"Last night . . . in God."*: HL, p. 141

CHAPTER 7: An Author in the Making
PAGE 73 *"When I write . . . revived!"*: AF, p. 247
PAGES 73–74 *"My fountain pen . . . thick nibs,"*: AF, p. 143
PAGE 74 *"She often said, . . . my diary,'"*: RFE, p. 139
PAGE 74 *"A few weeks ago . . . piling up,"*: RCE, p. 728
PAGE 75 *"Parts of . . . nothing special."*: RCE, p. 730
PAGE 76 *"If our descendants . . . a priest."*: RFE, p. 142
PAGE 76 *"When I write . . . revived!"*: AF, p. 247
PAGE 76 *"I'm my best . . . very much."*: AF, p. 247
PAGE 77 *"A bundle . . . my own secret."*: AF, p. 330
PAGE 77 *"I'm afraid . . . too weak."*: AF, p. 331

CHAPTER 8: Hope Betrayed
PAGE 79 *"I'm longing . . . inside me."*: AF, p. 184
PAGES 79–80 *"The period . . . her heart."*: AF, pp. 156–157
PAGE 80 *"I'm carrying . . . inside me."*: AF, p. 184
PAGE 80 *"obnoxious" and "a dope,"*: AF, p. 32
PAGE 80 *"gave [her] . . . blue eyes."*: AF, p. 160

PAGE 81 *"I go to . . . couldn't speak."*: AF, pp. 193–194

PAGE 82 *"Peter hasn't enough . . . and strength,"*: BIO, p. 216

PAGE 82 *"When I went . . . more information,"*: AFR, p. 183

PAGE 82 *"He called the day . . . 1944,"*: AFR, p. 184

PAGE 82 *"Will this year . . . there's life."*: AF, p. 307

PAGE 83 *"Vegetables . . . fit for a king!"*: AF, p. 277

PAGE 84 *"A few . . . his cheeks."*: AFR, p. 184

PAGE 84 *"It seemed . . . collapse,"*: AFR, p. 188

PAGE 84 *"Don't move,"*: AFR, p. 193

PAGE 84 *"Then we went . . . had arrived."*: AFH, pp. 178–79

PAGE 85 *"Anne walked . . . lost now,"*: RFE, p. xxi

PAGE 85 *"He turned it . . . loose pages,"*: AFH, p. 177

PAGE 86 *"Where did you get this?"*: AFH, pp. 177–78

PAGE 86 *"It belongs to me,"*: AFH, pp. 177–78

PAGE 86 *"You can . . . your time,"*: AFH, pp. 177–78

PAGE 87 *"I'll keep . . . comes back,"*: AFR, p. 199

CHAPTER 9: From the Annex to the Camps

PAGE 88 *"We are together . . . peace."*: RFE, p. 191

PAGE 88 *"You can't . . . to blame."*: FAF, p. 115

PAGE 89 *"Don't give . . . it differently."*: FAF, p. 115

PAGE 89 *"We knew . . . actually cheerful,"*: RFE, p. 154

PAGE 92 *"The freight cars . . . drowning,"*: RFE, p. 162

PAGE 93 *"The awful transportation . . . heads drop,"*: RFE, pp. 163–64

PAGES 93–94 *"Women . . . the right!"*: RFE, p. 167

PAGE 95 *"saw a group . . . their clothing."*: OF, p. 147

PAGE 96 *"We got a . . . last longer."*: LSM, pp. 60–61

PAGES 96–97 *"The biggest problem . . . about food."*: RFE, p. 176

PAGES 97–98 *"approaching the selection . . . the light."*: BIO, p. 252

PAGE 98 *"ill but . . . recovering"*: BIO, p. 252

PAGE 100 *"We watched . . . hold of,"*: RFE, p. 183

PAGE 101 *"So we stood . . . we cried,"*: LSM, p. 28

PAGES 102–103 *". . . At least . . . already wandering."*: RFE, p. 191

CHAPTER 10: The Aftermath

PAGE 105 *"I want . . . after my death!"*: AF, p. 247

PAGES 107–108 *"I began . . . feelings."*: RFE, p. 216

PAGE 111 *"We cannot . . . prejudice."*: OF, pp. 300–301

PAGE 112 *"I want to . . . inside me,"*: AF, p. 247

Chapter 11: What Happened to the Others?

PAGE 113 *"I believe . . . prejudice."*: OF, pp. 300–301

Image Credits

AP Images: 2, 5, 13, 21, 23, 37, 58, 59, 61, 80 (top and bottom)
Peter DeJong/AP Images: 71, 81
© Bettmann/Corbis: 6 (top), 9, 22, 25, 26, 64, 66, 85, 93, 94, 97, 111
© Dpa/Corbis: 106
© Todd Gipstein/Corbis: 112
© Hulton-Deutsch Collection/Corbis: 6 (bottom), 8, 46, 51, 68, 102
© Colin McPherson/Corbis: 115
© Nathan Benn/Corbis: 38
© Reuters/Corbis: 104
© Michael St. Maur Sheil/Corbis: 95
© Tetra Images/Corbis: 63
Max Bisschop/Maxey/www.flickr.com: 47
Ian Llyod/lloydi/www.flickr.com: 110
Getty Images: 7
Anne Frank House, Amsterdam/Getty Images: 30, 36, 44, 57
Anne Frank Fonds-Basel/Anne Frank House/Getty Images: 4, 11, 12, 16, 18, 34, 36, 40, 49, 56, 108
Koen Suyk/AFP/Getty Images: 88
Stan Honda/AFP/Getty Images: 29
East News/Getty Images: 107
Bernard Gotfryd/Getty Images: 114
Keystone/Getty Images: 52
Gali Tibbon/AFP/Getty Images: 78
George Rodger/Time & Life Pictures/Getty Images: 99, 103
The Granger Collection, New York: 14, 50, 62
ADN-Bildarchiv - ullstein bild/The Granger Collection, New York: 73
Rue des Archives/The Granger Collection, New York: 77
Library of Congress: 17, 54
National Archief, the Netherlands 935-0553: 76
National Archives and Records Administration: 91
National Monument Kamp Amersfoort: 90
Public Domain: 32, 75, 86
U.S. Coast Guard: 83
Courtesy of Betty Ann Wagner: 24
Daniel Ullrich/Wikipedia: 35
Cover art: Anne Frank Fonds-Basel/Anne Frank House, Amsterdam/Getty Images

About the Author

Rita Thievon Mullin lives in Alexandria, Virginia. She is the author of *Harry Houdini: Death Defying Showman* and *Thomas Jefferson: Architect of Freedom*—both part of the Sterling Biographies series—and of *Animalogy* and *Who's For Dinner?* When she is not writing books, she works in program development for a cable television channel.

Index

Ahlers, Tonny, 87
Amersfoort, 90
Amsterdam life, 12–23
  break-ins, 69–70
  building business, 10–11,
    20–22
  fate of Jews and, 66, 67
  Germany taking over, 26
  growing threats, 22–23,
    25–29
  home life, 18–20
  normalcy amidst turmoil,
    29–31
  school days, 14, 15–18,
    31–34
  SS actions, 65–67
Amsterdam, move to, 11, 12–
  13
Anne Frank House, 109–110
Annihilation, 104, 116
Anti-Semitism, 6–8, 22–23,
  116
Arrests, of annex residents,
  84–86, 87
Arrests/punishment, of
  helpers, 90
Atonement, 63, 116
Auschwitz-Birkenau, 92, 93–
  97, 105–106, 107
Beethoven, Ludwig van, 96,
  116
Bergen-Belsen, 97–103
Bicycles, 29, 35, 40, 41
Birth, of Anne, 2
Blackmailed, 87, 116
Black market, 69, 116
Blitz, Nanny (Nanette), 98–99
Bolkestein, Gerrit, 75–76
Brown Shirts, 8, 9, 116
Cat (Moortje), 31, 41, 43
Celebrations, in hiding, 62–63
Chancellor, 8, 116
Chestnut tree, 71
Childhood. See also
  Amsterdam life; Family life;
  Hiding, life in
  birth, 2
  loving stories, 4–5
  playing in mud, 4
  temperament, 3, 11
Concentration camps
  Amersfoort, 90
  Auschwitz-Birkenau, 92,
    93–97, 105–106, 107

avoiding, 1. See also Hiding,
  life in
Bergen-Belsen, 97–103
defined, 116
Dutch Jews sent to, 66
gas chambers in, 38
Holocaust and, 112
liberation of, 103, 105–
  106, 107
life in hell, 96–98
Polish Jews sent to, 85
selection process, 93–94
Westerbork, 89, 91–92
Crematoriums, 94, 95, 116
Curfews, 25
Death, of Anne, 103
Diaries, other, 78
Diary
  as dearest friend, 56–57
  entries, 42, 70–72, 76, 77,
    79–80, 81, 82, 83
  final entry, 77
  as gift, 1, 33–34
  growing compassion
    expressed in, 79–80
  Kitty and, 34, 74, 80, 82
  names in, 61
  notebooks/ledgers for, 53,
    74, 83
  Otto reading and
    publishing, 107–109
  photographs, 34, 77, 108
  prized pen for, 73–74
  rewriting for publication,
    76–77
  saving, 85, 86–87
  taking into hiding, 39
Dictator, 8, 116
Emigrated, 14, 114, 115, 116
Faith, consolation in, 70–72
Family life. See also Amsterdam
  life; Hiding, life in
  amidst Nazi rule, 9–11
  move to Netherlands, 10–
    11
Fear, living with, 64–72
Fiction, writing, 74–75
Final solution, 38, 104
Flowers, for Anne, 84
Food, securing, 50–53, 62,
  67–69, 82–83
Frank, Edith
  Anne criticizing, 79–80
  background and marriage, 3

death of, 98, 106
photograph, 80
planning for hiding, 36
shielding Anne and Margot,
  27, 29
Frank, Margot
  awareness of growing
    threat, 23
  to Bergen-Belsen, 97–103
  bicycle of, 35, 40, 41
  at Birkenau, 95–96
  illness/death, 101–103
  photograph, 23
  photographs, 5, 12, 13, 23,
    40
  reading and studying in
    hiding, 53
  rushed into hiding, 40–42
  temperament of, 2, 3
  work camp orders, 37–39
Frank, Otto
  on arrest, 86
  in Auschwitz, 95, 96–97,
    105–106
  building businesses, 10–11,
    20–22
  death of daughters and,
    106–107
  education, 3
  feeling guilty for arrest, 88–
    89
  life after war, 111
  life in New York, 3
  love of Anne, 19
  photographs, 5, 30, 56, 111
  protecting businesses from
    Germans, 27–28
  reading/publishing diary,
    107–109
  securing visas, 28–29
  storytelling of, 5
  on transport to Auschwitz,
    93
Frijda, Jetteke, 43
Gas chambers, 38
Geiringer, Eva, 31, 37, 111
Geiringer Frank, Fritzi, 111,
  113
Gies, Jan, 21, 27, 30, 39, 50–
  52, 54, 55, 61, 86, 107,
  113, 114
Gies, Miep
  buying flowers for Anne,
    83–84

Gies, Miep (*cont*)
  diary name, 61
  on effects of SS, 67
  Fritz Pfeffer and, 58, 59, 60
  Gestapo arrest and, 83–84
  hearing of Anne's death, 107
  helping hide families, 35,
    40, 41, 50–52, 55, 56, 67,
    69
  marriage to Jan, 30–31
  office duties, 20–21
  photographs, 21, 36, 56,
    114
  political views, 21
  postwar life, 113
  saved from arrest, 86
  saving diary, 86–87, 107
  supplying writing/reading
    materials, 53, 54, 74, 76,
    83
  on van Pels family, 22, 46
  on war progress, 82
Goldschmidt, Mr., 39, 41, 43
Good Paula and Bad Paula, 5
Goslar family, 20
Goslar, Hannah, 14–15, 16,
  19–20, 31, 32, 33, 34, 43,
  61, 70, 100–101, 114
Grandma Hollander, 11, 12,
  30–31, 73
Grandmother Frank, 27, 30,
  92, 113
Hartog-van Bladeren, Lena, 87
Hiding
  friends left behind, 43
  office staff helping with,
    35–36
  organizing space, 42
  preparing for, 35–37
  rushed into, 37–39, 40–42
Hiding, life in, 47–63
  adjusting to, 44–46
  bookcase access, 48–50
  break-ins, 69–70
  celebrations, 62–63
  church bell marking time,
    47–48
  consolation in faith, 70–72
  Dutch Resistance and, 50,
    51, 52
  end of, arrest and, 84–86,
    87
  hope for end of war, 82–84
  layout of space, 44, 48–50,
    57
  living with fear, 64–72
  reading passionately,
    53–54

  rising tensions, 59–60, 62
  securing food, 50–53, 62,
    67–69, 82–83
  visits from helpers, 45, 55–
    56
  who revealed, 87
Hitler, Adolf, rise to power, 6–
  9
Hollander, Julius and Walter,
  10, 28, 114
Holocaust, 104, 112
Hooligan, 8, 116
Joop, book series, 32, 34
Kiss, first, 81
Kitty, 34, 74, 80, 82
Kleiman, Jo (Johannes), 22,
  27, 35–36, 48, 56, 61, 65,
  66, 84, 86, 88–89, 90, 114
Kugler, Victor, 20, 27, 35–36,
  48–50, 55, 56, 61, 84, 86,
  90
Laskier, Rutka, 78
Lederman, Sanne (Susanne),
  14–15, 30, 31, 32, 33, 34,
  61, 114
Legacy of Anne Frank, 1, 112
Love, first, 80–82. *See also* Van
  Pels, Peter
Lueger, Karl, 7
Margot. *See* Frank, Margot
Master race, 6–8
Mathews, Birdie, 24
Miep. *See* Gies, Miep
Montessori school, 15–16, 17,
  18
National Socialist German
  Workers' Party. *See* Nazis
Nazis, 1
  anti-Semitism of, 6–8, 22–
    23, 116
  defined, 116
  National Socialist German
    Workers' Party as, 6
  SS actions in Netherlands,
    65–67
  sympathizers, 9, 117
Otto. *See* Frank, Otto
Palestine, 100, 116
Parents. *See* Frank, Edith;
  Frank, Otto
Parks, Jews banned from, 29–
  30
Pen pals, 23, 24
Pension, 44, 116
Pfeffer, Fritz, 58, 59–60, 61,
  92, 96, 97
Photos, of Anne, 5, 11, 13, 14,
  16, 18, 30, 61, 73, 75

Prisoner exchange program,
  100
Rabble-rousing, 9, 116
Radio reports, 25, 27, 45, 46,
  57, 67, 82
Ration coupons/cards/books,
  26, 50–52, 67
Religion, consolation in, 70–72
Religious holidays, 63
Resistance, 50, 51, 52, 116
Sabbath, 20, 63, 70, 116
Schiff, Peter, 33, 61, 80, 115
School days, 14, 15–18, 31–
  34
Schubert, Franz, 96, 116
Secret annex. *See* Hiding, life
  in
Silberbauer, Karl Joseph, 85–
  86, 87
Silberberg, Helmuth "Hello,"
  37, 39, 43, 61, 115
Storytelling, 4–5
Streetcar, 11, 116
Sympathizer, 9, 117
Synagogue, 33, 63, 70, 117
Theaters, Jews banned from,
  29, 33
Thirteenth birthday, 1, 33–34
Van Maaren, William, 87
Van Maarsen, Jacque
  (Jacqueline), 32, 33, 34,
  36, 43, 61, 115
Van Pels, Auguste, 36, 48, 59,
  61, 69, 95, 99–100, 101
Van Pels, Hermann, 22, 36, 37,
  48, 55, 59, 61, 69, 95
Van Pels, Peter, 36, 45–46, 48,
  49, 53, 59, 61, 80–82, 84–
  85, 95, 96, 105, 106
Visas, 28–29, 117
Voskuijl, Elly (Bep), 30, 35,
  36, 48, 50, 52–53, 55, 56,
  61, 67, 74, 76, 83, 84, 86,
  115
Westerbork, 89, 91–92
Wijnberg, Hans and Els, 69–
  70
Wilhelmina, Queen of
  Netherlands, 26, 27, 46
Work camps, 36–37, 38. *See
  also* Concentration camps
World War I, effects of, 5–6
World War II
  hope for end of, 82–84, 89
  overview, 68

Discover interesting personalities
in the Sterling Biographies® series:

Marian Anderson: *A Voice Uplifted*
Neil Armstrong: *One Giant Leap for Mankind*
Alexander Graham Bell: *Giving Voice to the World*
Cleopatra: *Egypt's Last and Greatest Queen*
Christopher Columbus: *The Voyage That Changed the World*
Jacques Cousteau: *A Life Under the Sea*
Davy Crockett: *Frontier Legend*
Marie Curie: *Mother of Modern Physics*
Frederick Douglass: *Rising Up from Slavery*
Amelia Earhart: *A Life in Flight*
Thomas Edison: *The Man Who Lit Up the World*
Albert Einstein: *The Miracle Mind*
Anne Frank: *Hidden Hope*
Benjamin Franklin: *Revolutionary Inventor*
Matthew Henson: *The Quest for the North Pole*
Harry Houdini: *Death-Defying Showman*
Thomas Jefferson: *Architect of Freedom*
Joan of Arc: *Heavenly Warrior*
Helen Keller: *Courage in Darkness*
John F. Kennedy: *Voice of Hope*
Martin Luther King, Jr.: *A Dream of Hope*
Lewis & Clark: *Blazing a Trail West*
Abraham Lincoln: *From Pioneer to President*
Rosa Parks: *Courageous Citizen*
Eleanor Roosevelt: *A Courageous Spirit*
Franklin Delano Roosevelt: *A National Hero*
Harriet Tubman: *Leading the Way to Freedom*
George Washington: *An American Life*
The Wright Brothers: *First in Flight*
Malcolm X: *A Revolutionary Voice*